WISDOM

TIMELESS TREASURES FROM PROVERBS

GERALD WHEELER

REVIEW AND HERALD® PUBLISHING ASSOCIATION
HAGERSTOWN, MD 21740

This book was
Edited by Richard W. Coffen
Copyedited by Jocelyn Fay and James Cavil
Designed by Bill Tymeson
Typeset: 11/13 Minion

PRINTED IN U.S.A.

03 02 01 00   5 4 3 2 1

R&H Cataloging Service
Wheeler, Gerald William, 1943-
      Wisdom: Timeless treasures from Proverbs

      1. Bible. O.T. Proverbs—Commentaries. I. Title

ISBN 0-8280-1527-9

To order additional copies of
Wisdom: Timeless Treasures From Proverbs
by Gerald Wheeler, call:
1-800-765-6955
View us at *www.rhpa.org* for information
on Review and Herald products.

DEDICATED TO

Austin Beachley, craftsman

CONTENTS

Chapter One

WISDOM—THE PATH TO LIFE

Family counselors and psychologists tell us that the stories a family shares with each other reveal much about the members themselves. Such anecdotes reflect the values, dreams, fears, loves, hatreds, and a host of other things about the family. Family tales indicate relationships—who is honored, who is an outcast, what the family as a whole expects of those who belong to it. The stories that circulate about Uncle Joe, Aunt Sarah, or Great-grandfather Mel perhaps disclose more about the rest of the family than they do the person being talked about.

Mottoes, sayings, and proverbs also point to what a family considers important. They articulate philosophies and values, indicating how people would like to live even if they don't quite measure up to the maxim. The grandmother who constantly quotes Proverbs 6:6 about the ant storing away food for the future is reflecting her own life struggles and dreams to succeed.

Unfortunately, it is easy for an adage to lose its impact. People can quote something, but not necessarily live up to its philosophy. They promote an ideal but lack the power to put it into action, to bring it into reality. Or individuals may do the exact opposite of what they espouse, using the saying as a means to impress, deceive, or cover up their shortcomings.

In English the term *platitude* has acquired a negative sense. In everyday usage it connotes something dull and obvious, perhaps even deceptive. Politicians and leaders of all kinds quote them—but never follow them. Thus platitude has become a pejorative, a dismissal, or even a hostile rejection of what someone says. It has almost become a synonym for a lie.

Sadly, this attitude has often marked people's reaction to the biblical book of Proverbs. They see its sayings as dull, superficial, and irrelevant to real life, because nobody actually puts them into practice. Christians, especially, sometimes dismiss them as even legalistic—as promoting a philosophy of trying to be good on one's own. The book of Proverbs might offer good common sense, but it is irrelevant to the gospel. Perhaps that may be one reason early Christian interpreters did not comment on the book as a whole even though they were interested in some individual sayings or sections, especially Proverbs 31:10-31.[1] Too many people regard the book of Proverbs as a grab bag full of homespun aphorisms that have no theological depth or significance.

What Is a Proverb?

The book of Proverbs consists of individual sayings and extended poems. The separate sayings often seem to be strung together by a catchphrase or very loosely developed themes.[2] In chapter 24, for example, the themes include such topics as conduct in court (Prov. 24:24, 25, 28); speaking and thinking (verses 26, 28); and attitudes toward work (verses 27, 30-34). Sometimes the same theme will show up in several places in the book. The Hebrew word *mashal*, translated "proverb," has a much broader meaning than its English equivalent. It is rendered "taunt" in Isaiah 14:4, "oracle" in Numbers 23:7 and 18, and "allegory" in Ezekiel 17:2. The term comes from a verb standing for "to be like" or "to resemble."[3]

Scholars have seen *mashal* as containing the concept of "comparison."[4]

Some of the passages in Proverbs appear to be true folk sayings, while others are more academic in tone. Chapters 1-9 are more discursive, elaborating and building upon a thought, than the pithy sayings found in the rest of the book.

The maxims employ highly figurative language, using metaphors and other imagery and symbolism. In the Hebrew language the proverbs contain extensive alliteration and like to play on sounds—they're puns. Often passages follow a chiastic pattern in which the first half is a mirror image of the second half. The most common literary characteristic is that of parallelism. Parallelism involves either repeating a thought in a succeeding line, or expanding it in some way. Scholars generally recognize three main forms of parallelism: synonymous, antithetical, or synthetic.

1. In synonymous parallelism the second line or clause repeats the first in different words:

(a) "The evil bow down before the good,

(b) the wicked at the gates of the righteous" (Prov. 14:19).

(a) "Pride goes before destruction,

(b) and a haughty spirit before a fall" (Prov. 16:18).

2. The most common form of parallelism is the antithetical saying. The second line contrasts with the first, usually taking the reverse perspective:

(a) "The wise woman builds her house,

(b) but the foolish tears it down with her own hands" (Prov. 14:1).

(a) "Whoever is slow to anger has great understanding,

(b) but one who has a hasty temper exalts folly" (verse 29).

Throughout Proverbs the sayings set wisdom and the wise in opposition to folly and the fool. By the way, fools in this context are not mentally deficient. They can be quite intelligent. Rather, they lack self-control and exhibit their deficiency in anger, arrogance, self-centeredness, inability to control their emotions, destructive behavior, rebelliousness, and a host of other negative traits.[5] The wise may not have greater intelligence, but they "fear the Lord, and turn away from evil" (Prov. 3:7). The "fear of the Lord" is humanity's proper response to God, and that involves awe, reverence, trust, obedience, and service.[6]

3. Sayings falling into the synthetic parallelism classification have the second line continuing the thought of the first, expanding or building upon it:

    (a) "The fear of the Lord is a fountain of life,
    (b) so that one may avoid the snares of death" (Prov. 14:27).

    (a) "Those with good sense are slow to anger,
    (b) and it is to their glory to overlook an offense" (Prov. 19:11).

In addition, the book has such kinds of sayings as the "not good" (example: Prov. 19:2), "abomination" (example: Prov. 11:1), "better" (example: Prov. 22:1), and numerical (X number plus 1; example: Prov. 30:18, 19). The parabolic distich relates several factual elements to a moral concept (for example, Prov. 26:3).

The various proverbs in the book fall into two main categories: sayings and admonitions. Sayings, on the one hand, reflect life as experienced—that which the biblical writer has observed. Such passages do not tell readers what they must or must not do but just record things as they are. Example: "A slack hand causes poverty, but the hand of the diligent makes rich" (Prov. 10:4). An admonition, on the other hand, urges its audience to do or not to do something. Example: "Do not rob the poor because they are poor, or crush the afflicted at the gate; for the Lord pleads their cause and despoils of life those who despoil them" (Prov. 22:22, 23). The proverbs can be individual sayings, or they can form extended didactic poems as found in Proverbs 22 and 31.

The Structure of the Book

The various proverbs belong to a series of collections of sayings organized along the following structure:

Outline of the Book of Proverbs
   I. "The Proverbs of Solomon Son of David, king of Israel" (wisdom poems) (Prov. 1:1-9:18)
  II. Wisdom sayings (Prov. 10:1-22:16)
 III. Admonitions (Prov. 22:17-24:22)
  IV. "Sayings of the Wise" (Prov. 24:23-34)
   V. "Proverbs of Solomon" (Prov. 25:1-29:7)
  VI. "The Words of Agur" (Prov. 30:1-33)
 VII. "The Words of King Lemuel's Mother" (Prov. 31:1-9)
VIII. Ode to a virtuous woman or ideal wife (Prov. 31:10-31)[7]

When the average person hears of the book of Proverbs, he or she automatically thinks of Solomon as author of all of it. The book does claim Solomonic authorship for specific parts (Prov. 1:1; 10:1; 24:25).[8] First Kings 3:9-12 and 4:29-34 portray Solomon's desire for wisdom and his composition of many proverbs. Yet the book itself lists several other possible additional authors. Proverbs 30:1-33 has the heading "The Words of Agur" and states that Agur is the son of Jakeh. A Jewish midrash identified Agur with Solomon, who "stored up" (*agar*) wisdom and "spewed it out" (*hiqqi* = Jakeh) by taking many wives. Another ancient tradition equated Agur with Solomon and Jakeh with David. The name Agur does appear in Sabean Arabic inscriptions, however.[9] But the Septuagint and Vulgate translations appear to suggest that their translators were not sure if Agur was a proper name.[10]

The name Lemuel in Proverbs 31:1 is Hebrew for "belonging to God." The Septuagint translated it with the Greek "spoken by God." But if we accept the verse at face value, the sayings of verses 2-9 do not come from Lemuel, but a woman, his mother. In addition, we have the ambiguous references to the

"Sayings of the Wise" (Prov. 24:23) and "Further Sayings of the Wise" (Prov. 25:1). These various sections were brought together as a single book no earlier than the time of Hezekiah (Prov. 25:1), who lived centuries after the time of Solomon.[11] (In this book to simplify things we will refer to the author as the biblical sage, scribe, or writer no matter which part of the book we are examining.)

Solomon could not have originated all of Proverbs 24:23-34 because we find close parallels in an Egyptian document called *Instruction of Amenemope* that dates centuries before his birth.[12] The reason we find such parallels between the *Instruction of Amenemope* and Proverbs is that they both belong to a widespread literary genre known as wisdom literature.

The World of Wisdom Literature

What scholars call wisdom literature ranged across the ancient Near East from Egypt to Mesopotamia. Recording the attempts of human beings to understand the meaning of life, it existed long before the composition of the Bible.

All ancient wisdom writings began with three fundamental assumptions.

1. Wisdom was practical rather than theoretical. It dealt with the things of everyday life as opposed to some arcane knowledge. Thus a wise person knew how to rule well, a craftsperson knew how to do his trade well, and a wise woman knew how to manage her household well.

2. Wisdom belonged to the gods, who delivered it to humanity through their chosen agents.

3. Wisdom, when given to humanity, rested in such earthly institutions or authorities as kings, scribes and their writings, and the heads of households.[13]

We find these three concepts also displayed in the book of Proverbs. In it, though, the source of wisdom is the only true God.

Egyptian wisdom writings most often took the form of a father giving advice and warnings to his son. The book of

Proverbs echoes this in its frequent use of the phrase "my son."
The Egyptian wisdom writers constantly said "Do this" or "Do
not do that" in their instructions. Proverbs also follows this
style. The *Instruction of Ptahhotep* (dating perhaps back to the
Sixth Dynasty, 2400-2200 B.C.), for example, has the father declare to his son:

> "If you meet a disputant in action,
>
> A poor man, not your equal,
>
> Do not attack him because he is weak,
>
> Let him alone, he will confute himself.
>
> Do not answer him to relieve your heart,
>
> Do not vent yourself against your opponent." [14]

Mesopotamian wisdom literature usually consisted of collections of short proverbs and sayings that simply describe life
as it is. [15] As mentioned earlier, this is also the most frequent literary form in the biblical book of Proverbs. Even beyond that,
we find similarities in content and thought with Mesopotamian
wisdom. The *Words of Ahiqar*, to cite one example, was com-
posed in Assyria about the time of the Israelite monarchy and,
as we shall see in chapter 13, has many sayings closely parallel-
ing those in the book of Proverbs. Interestingly, we know that
at least some Jews were aware of *Ahiqar* because an Aramaic
translation of it was found among the documents of the fifth-
century Jewish military colony stationed on the island of
Elephantine in Upper Egypt. Throughout the rest of this study
on Proverbs we shall note in passing some of the parallels between Proverbs and nonbiblical wisdom writings.

Both the Egyptian and Mesopotamian wisdom literature advocate patterns of behavior that if dutifully followed would
start the reader on the road to a long, happy, and successful career. The student of wisdom learned that an all-pervading divine order governed the world. To be successful one must obey
that order in every aspect of life. To ignore or go against it
would lead to disaster. A passage in the *Instruction of Ptahhotep*
summarizes the wisdom tradition's approach: "Truth (that is,

the Order) is good and of permanent value, and has remained unchanged since the day when it was created. Whoever breaks its rules is punished. It lies before the uninstructed like a straight path. Wrongdoing has never yet brought its undertakings safe home to port. Evil may indeed acquire wealth, but the strength of truth lies in its permanence, and the righteous man says, 'It is an inheritance from my father.'"[16]

Egyptians called that order *maat*. They represented it by a goddess with a feather in her hair. Just the image of a feather by itself could also symbolize *maat*. Individual Egyptians believed that they would be judged by whether or not they had lived according to *maat*. Artists portrayed the deceased standing before the god Anubis as he weighed their hearts in a balance. The heart, the ancient symbol of the human mind or consciousness, rested in one pan of the balance and the feather of *maat* in the other.

The ancients saw such world order as external even to the gods. The deities were subject to the principles of the universe instead of the other way around. Order was more powerful than the gods themselves.

God Speaks in a Culture's Language

The parallels between Proverbs and the nonbiblical wisdom literature can be disturbing to some. Their unease can grow when they encounter still other similarities between nonbiblical documents and additional parts of Scripture. Consider these examples from a New Kingdom stela from Deir-el-Medina:

"You are Amen, the Lord of the silent, who pays heed to the voice of the poor. When I call to you in my distress you come to rescue me. You give breath to me in my wretchedness and release me from my bondage."[17]

"The Lord is disposed to forgive.
The Lord of Thebes spends not a whole day in anger,
His wrath passes in a moment, none remains.
His breath comes back to us in mercy,
Amun returns upon his breeze."[18]

If you substituted Yahweh for Amen, you might mistake these quotations as coming from the psalms. How can we explain the similarities between the way Israel described its God and the way Egyptians referred to their deities? As we consider what appears to be biblical borrowing, we must keep several factors in mind.

1. To speak to a culture, one must use the language—the imagery and concepts—of that culture. It takes familiar images and ideas as well as words to communicate. Anyone who has tried to read a computer manual recognizes the difficulty of understanding something that employs not only unknown words but unfamiliar concepts and allusions as well.

Bible translators particularly have to struggle with this problem. The only four-legged mammal the people of Papua New Guinea knew for a long time was the pig. Sheep do not live on the tropical island. How, then, does one translate the biblical phrase "lamb of God"? The image of sheep is totally unknown, thus has no meaning for them. As a result, some missionaries used the image of "the pig of God." Startling as it may be to most Christians, it does communicate something to a people not only familiar with pigs but also who value them highly. After the Papuan has grasped the underlying concept, the Christian missionary can then introduce the new convert to the fact that Scripture compares Christ to a lamb. But just showing the Papuan a photograph of a strange longhaired creature does not as easily get across the idea of something valuable and beloved.

During what scholars call the First Intermediate Period of Egyptian history (c. 2200-2050 B.C.), a son put an inscribed jar stand in his father's tomb. The message on the stand had several requests that the son hoped the father would intercede with the gods in the afterlife about, including a plea that a healthy male child would be born to the son. The son told his deceased father, "As you live for me, may the Great One [perhaps the goddess Hathor] favor you and the face of the Great God be kindly disposed toward you and he give you pure bread from his two hands."[19]

Most likely the saying was a common one in Egyptian culture. Centuries later the God of Israel told Moses to have Aaron and his sons use the familiar phrase as a blessing for His people (Num. 6:22-26). Since His people had spent generations in Egypt, He knew that the concept would be meaningful to them.

2. The fact that the Bible employs extrabiblical imagery does not necessarily mean that there is any direct borrowing from pagan documents. The imagery may be just something that Israel shared with the rest of the ancient world. Some scholars have argued that Psalm 104 borrowed heavily from the Egyptian Hymn to Aten. Both have some striking imagery and phrasing in common.[20] James K. Hoffmeier traced some of the imagery in the Hymn to Aten and found that it appeared in Egyptian literature and iconography centuries before the time of Akhenaten.[21] It appears that both the Hymn to Aten and Psalm 104 used imagery that was widespread in the ancient Near East, imagery that long predated both documents.[22] Such imagery was a handy tool to communicate certain topics.

3. Just because both biblical and nonbiblical passages use the same imagery or even phrasing does not mean that they are saying the same thing. Many years ago Helmer Ringgren cautioned that "the same expression, when used in different religious literatures, does not always mean the same thing. Thus two similar phrases do not necessarily convey identical ideas. It is sufficient to recall the differing connotations of such words as 'peace,' 'freedom,' and 'democracy' in the Western world and in communist countries. Attention must therefore be paid to the whole religious and cultural environment in which an expression or religious practice occurs."[23]

Thus the important thing to consider is not what is borrowed, but what the biblical writer did with it. We must carefully determine what the imagery or material taken from the world around Israel now says when placed in the new context. We must always ask ourselves How has it been changed, modified, or transformed? Even an old metaphor, allusion, or illustration can be given a new twist that radically changes its meaning.

4. Finally, God is the author of truth no matter where we find it (cf. Rom. 1:20; Ps. 19:1-4). If we find religious truth in pagan religious writings, it ultimately had its source in God. Whether He reveals it through direct revelation or just through commonsense observation, only God can help us to recognize and understand truth. And, if nothing else, it takes divine wisdom to recognize wisdom in any culture.

The book of Proverbs sometimes uses imagery and concepts known throughout the ancient Near East, but it weaves them into new understandings and insights—the most important being each individual's need for a personal relationship with the God who governs everything in the universe. "In the polytheistic systems of Egypt and Mesopotamia there was a multiplicity of gods, none of whom was by himself in supreme control of the universe, and the Order to which men were expected to conform was distant from and superior to the gods— an impersonal force. But the Israelite's conviction that everything in heaven and earth was under the control of his God, Yahweh, . . . enabled him, in the end, to see more clearly than his neighbours the true relationship between wisdom and religious faith. . . . Wisdom is first and foremost the possession of God himself." [24]

Space does not permit us to do a verse-by-verse commentary of Proverbs. Instead we will explore only a few selected themes from among the many in the book.

Distinctive Concepts in Proverbs

Although at times the book of Proverbs may echo some ideas held in common with the rest of the ancient Near East, it weaves them into a pattern of specific ideas that form a unique understanding of what wisdom involves. Richard J. Clifford focuses on what he sees as five major theses of the biblical book. [25]

1. God made the world so that it rewards good deeds and punishes bad ones. The Lord is vitally concerned about justice, and what people do has real consequences.

2. Wisdom is not just knowledge or skill, but includes justice and piety. Religion and ethics are as important as what we know.

3. Human beings have great freedom in what they do. Instead of being the puppets of fate or other blind forces, they are free moral agents. Wisdom's ideal is that when people once know good, they will then do it themselves.

4. Life consists of either walking in the path of righteousness or following the path of evil, usually referred to as the way of folly. Although the idea of two paths or ways does appear in other wisdom traditions, Proverbs develops it into a major theme.

5. The book of Proverbs uses antithetical or contrasting types to describe behavior and the consequences of those actions. The biblical writer, for example, pairs the righteous and the wicked, the industrious and the slothful, and the rich and the poor.

Concern for Righteousness

The book of Proverbs also probes deeper into human behavior than does the wisdom literature of the surrounding cultures. It is concerned with more than just external success. The sage is interested in what Scripture calls righteousness. Proverbs uses the Hebrew word for righteousness (sedeq) more times than any other Old Testament book.[26]

Sun Myung Lyu sees the biblical book as inculcating righteousness by instructing its readers on how to form good characters. Righteousness is charity and compassion, and righteous people emulate the God of justice. But as they do so, they are totally dependent on God Himself. The righteous demonstrate in their behavior how others should seek to become righteous. The righteous are moral and spiritual examples and role models for the rest of society.

The ultimate role model of the righteous person would

come in the person of Jesus. His life on earth would show humanity what righteousness truly was like. He demonstrated that the righteous life was one of caring and justice. The book of Proverbs had seen the righteous as wooing fellow human beings to righteousness. Jesus became the ultimate wooer, drawing humanity to the righteousness He so lovingly portrayed.

The Search for Wisdom

The book of Proverbs begins by announcing the benefits it will bring to its readers.[27]

Proverbs, echoing Deuteronomy 30:16, 19, offers wisdom and instruction (Prov. 1:2), teaches wise dealing, righteousness, justice, and equity (verse 3), and brings shrewdness to the simple[28] and knowledge to the young (verse 4). It will accomplish these things by enabling its audience to see the meanings couched in proverbial sayings and metaphorical language— "the words of the wise and their riddles" (verses 5, 6). They must "listen"—one of the most frequently used verbs in wisdom literature and standing for obedience.[29]

Egyptian wisdom writings also emphasize listening, as we see in the epilogue to the *Instruction of Ptahhotep*.[30] The biblical sage declares that knowledge begins with the "fear of the Lord," a refrain throughout the book (cf. Prov. 9:10; 15:33) and elsewhere in Scripture (Ex. 3:6; 19; Deut. 5:5; Job 28:28; Ps. 111:10). It is obedience to God's will as revealed through the religion of Israel. On the other hand, fools[31] refuse to listen and learn (Prov. 1:7).

Proverbs 1:20-23 personifies wisdom as a woman who goes out into the marketplace and advertises to everyone. She gives an impassioned appeal. Wisdom is not restricted to the elect, the privileged, however. Dame Wisdom, as Roland E. Murphy likes to call her, wants all to possess wisdom, especially the simple,[32] the scoffers, and the fools (verse 22). If they will but listen, "I will pour out my thoughts to you; I will make my words known to you" (verse 23).

Wisdom does not come to the passive or apathetic. Not only must it be responded to (Prov. 2:1, 2), but also wisdom requires effort to acquire it (verses 3, 4). Human beings must dig for it as miners tunnel through the rock for silver or other treasure (verse 4). In fact, it is more valuable than all other riches. Verse 5 equates "the fear of the Lord" and "the knowledge of God" by placing them in parallel with each other. But even though humanity may have to struggle to get wisdom, it comes only from God. Only He can reveal it, for "from his mouth come knowledge and understanding" (verse 6).

The God of wisdom will "shield" those who walk in His ways and preserve them (verses 7, 8). He will ensure justice (verse 8), partly because those with wisdom will understand what justice and righteousness really are (verse 10). God-given understanding and knowledge will protect their recipient from evil both within and outside (verses 11, 12). It will especially shield God's children from human agents of sin and evil (verses 12-19). Both here in verses 18, 19 and in Proverbs 9:14-18 "Woman Folly" (Dame Wisdom's opposite) has a house, and her guests are in Sheol. God's children can face no greater danger than spiritual death. (In chapters 4 and 12 we will look at the literal problem the imagery of the adulteress is based upon.)

Proverbs 2:20 describes the life of wisdom as a walk along a path, an image that also appears in nonbiblical wisdom. Again we see that the spiritual life is not passive, but is active and has direction to it. The path is a frequent image in the book of Proverbs.

The sage in Proverbs 3:13-18 declares that wisdom is the greatest possible wealth, bringing incalculable rewards with her. She is better than silver and gold and more valuable than jewels (verses 14, 15). Nothing can compare with wisdom (verse 15). Dame Wisdom brings long life, riches, and honor (verse 16),[33] and her ways are pleasant and peaceful (verse 17). In verse 18 the sage uses a favorite biblical image that was also widespread throughout the ancient Near East—the tree of life. Those who cling to Dame Wisdom will find true happiness.

Proverbs 4 employs the image of a father making an impassioned plea for his child to find and accept wisdom. He describes how he obtained wisdom himself from his own father (verses 3, 4), so he knows what he is talking about. Thus his own children should trust him when he emphatically declares, "Get wisdom; get insight" (verse 5). If his children will not abandon wisdom, but love her, she will keep and guard them (verse 6). Give her the value she deserves, and she will bring honor (something greatly desired in biblical culture) (verse 8). In verses 10-13 the wisdom poem returns to the imagery of the path—or way—of wisdom. Should the child accept the father's teachings, the reward will be long life (verse 10), once more echoing Deuteronomy 30:16, 19. The wise follow the path that divine wisdom charts. It is a path in which one may run without stumbling (verse 12).[34]

"Keep hold of instruction," the father exhorts his children, "do not let go; guard her, for she is your life" (verse 13).

Proverbs 8 returns to the imagery of Dame Wisdom going to the gate, the site of the marketplace and the most public spot in any ancient city (verses 1-3). Unlike chapter 1, though, chapter 8 speaks of personified Wisdom in the third person. She summons the "simple" to learn prudence and those who need intelligence to acquire it from her (verse 5). The woman Wisdom declares that she will speak only truth and righteousness. Wickedness is an abomination to her (verses 6-8). Again she announces that wisdom's instruction is more valuable than gold, silver, or jewels (verses 10, 11). She represents integrity itself.

The book of Proverbs repeatedly stresses that wisdom is beyond value. Those who follow "the path of Wisdom will be blessed with every kind of happiness, including that brought by worldly goods, whereas the man who ignores Wisdom and makes only for riches will in the end be disappointed of both."[35] She offers good advice, insight, and strength (verse 14).

True wisdom is free from the faults of the world's wisdom. It has the fear of the Lord. All those who reverence God will naturally reject pride, arrogance, perverted speech, and all wickedness (verse 13). Dame Wisdom enables rulers to govern justly and well (verses 15, 16). Everyone who seeks and accepts her will find themselves showered with wealth and honor (verses 18-21) far beyond that dreamed by those who sought wisdom in nonbiblical cultures. She walks in the way of what the Egyptians would have called Order *(Maat)* but what the God of Israel referred to as righteousness (verse 20). When God's people find wisdom, they will be in harmony not only with the universe but with God Himself.

In Proverbs 9 Dame Wisdom holds a banquet and calls all who will to feast with her. In the biblical world eating was an intimate occasion between host and guest. Here we must be in intimate union with Dame Wisdom. She, like the host in Christ's parable of the wedding supper, sends out servants to summon her guests. The guests' need, or deficiency, is their only qualification to attend.[36] But they must lay aside their immaturity and walk in the way of insight, or wisdom (verse 6). The chapter goes on to remind us once more that the beginning of wisdom is the fear of the Lord, and it defines that as "knowledge of the Holy One" (verse 10). Wisdom never exists by itself, but only in relation to God. To know God—that is true wisdom.

The biblical sage constantly emphasizes why it is important to have wisdom. For example, wickedness can never provide security, but those who have wisdom will have the stability of the most deeply-rooted tree (Prov. 12:3). While the house of those who do evil will eventually collapse, the house of the righteous— those who possess wisdom—will continue to stand (verse 7), able to withstand the flash floods and earthquakes of life. By house, the sage here means "household," "everything precious to the individual, making it possible for him to truly live."[37] Jesus would elaborate on this imagery in Matthew 7:24-27.

Wisdom is not esoteric knowledge or the *gnosis* of some early Christian cults. As we have already noted, it cannot exist apart from God, but is a reflection of who He is and how He relates to everything else. The Egyptians thought of themselves as being judged against *maat*. But the God of the Bible evaluates our lives by His. He may substitute Christ's character for ours in the final judgment, but the criterion is still the divine character, not some impersonal external order of things. Going beyond ancient Near Eastern wisdom, the wisdom of Scripture is infinitely more than being in harmony with the order of the universe. It is being in an obedient, loving relationship with the God of the universe. As Proverbs 8 intimates and the New Testament most fully reveals, it is a divine-human love relationship empowered by God Himself. It is a relationship between God, who loves us to the point of dying in our place, and those of us who allow ourselves to respond to that infinite love. When we open ourselves to Him, He will give us the ability to live out the principles of the book of Proverbs.

---

[1] Roland E. Murphy, *Proverbs*, Word Biblical Commentary (Nashville: Thomas Nelson, 1998), p. xxvii.

[2] For a more detailed examination of how the book of Proverbs weaves together catchwords and ideas, see David A. Dorsey, *The Literary Structure of the Old Testament: A Commentary on Genesis-Malachi* (Grand Rapids: Baker Book House, 1999), pp. 187-191.

[3] R. K. Harrison, *Introduction to the Old Testament* (Grand Rapids: Eerdmans, 1969), pp. 1010, 1011.

[4] Roland E. Murphy, *The Tree of Life: An Exploration of Biblical Wisdom Literature* (New York: Doubleday, 1990), p. 7.

[5] See Leland Ryken, James C. Wilhot, Tremper Longman III, eds., *Dictionary of Biblical Imagery* (Downers Grove, Ill.: InterVarsity Press, 1998), pp. 296, 297.

[6] *Ibid.*, pp. 277, 278.

[7] The Septuagint arranged the sayings in a somewhat different order than that found in Bibles today (Harrison, p. 1019).

[8] Rabbinical tradition apparently assigned Proverbs to Hezekiah and placed the book chronologically after Psalms and Job, but the Septuagint grouped it with Ecclesiastes and the Song of Solomon so that all the books considered to be by Solomon would be together. See Harrison, p. 1010.

[9] David Noel Freedman, ed., *Anchor Bible Dictionary* (New York: Doubleday, 1992), vol. 1, p. 100.

[10] Geoffrey W. Bromiley, ed., *The International Standard Bible Encyclopedia* (Grand Rapids: Eerdmans, 1979), vol. 1, p. 75.

[11] Harrison, pp. 1017, 1018.

[12] Even the conservative scholar R. K. Harrison considers the connection indisputable (see his *Introduction to the Old Testament*, pp. 1013-1017). Much has been written on the parallels between Proverbs and the Egyptian document. See Murphy, *Proverbs*, pp. 290-294; Derek Kidner, *Proverbs: An Introduction and Commentary* (Leicester, Eng.: InterVarsity Press, 1964), pp. 23, 24; R.B.Y. Scott, *Proverbs/Ecclesiastes*, pp. xii, xiii; John H. Walton, *Ancient Israelite Literature in Its Cultural Context: A Survey of Parallels Between Biblical and Ancient Near Eastern Texts* (Grand Rapids: Zondervan, 1989), pp. 192-197. Walton parallels the passages from Proverbs with *Amenemope*, as does R. N. Whybray, *The Book of Proverbs*, Cambridge Bible Commentary (London: Cambridge University Press, 1972). Whybray compares them point by point (pp. 132-141). He suggests that Proverbs echoes only the first part of *Amenemope*. D. Winton Thomas, ed., *Documents From Old Testament Times* (New York: Harper and Row, 1958) and Victor H. Matthews and Don C. Benjamin, *Old Testament Parallels: Laws and Stories From the Ancient Near East* (New York: Paulist Press, 1991) also indicate the correspondences between *Amenemope* and Proverbs. Richard J. Clifford suggests how the biblical writers may have adapted ancient Near Eastern wisdom sayings for their own purposes (*Proverbs: A Commentary* [Louisville: Westminster John Knox Press, 1998], pp. 17-19).

[13] Clifford, pp. 8, 9.

[14] Miriam Lichtheim, *Ancient Egyptian Literature* (Berkeley, Calif.: University of California Press, 1973), Vol. I, p. 64.

[15] For the background of Mesopotamian parallels, see Clifford, pp. 9-17.

[16] Whybray, p. 8. Cf. Lichtheim's translation, p. 64.

[17] Quoted in Joyce Tyldesley, *Daughters of Isis: Women of Ancient Egypt* (London: Penguin Books, 1995), pp. 246, 247. Cf. Miriam Lichtheim's translation in her *Ancient Egyptian Literature* (Berkeley, Calif.: University of California Press, 1976), Vol. II, p. 106.

[18] Lichtheim, Vol. II, p. 107.

[19] *Letters From Ancient Egypt.* Edmund S. Meltzer, ed. Edward F. Wente, trans. (Atlanta: Scholars Press, 1990), p. 213.

[20] See Thomas, pp. 142-150; Matthews and Benjamin, pp. 153-156; and James B. Pritchard, ed., *Ancient Near Eastern Texts Relative to the Old Testament* (Princeton, N.J.: Princeton University Press, 1955), p. 370.

[21] James K. Hoffmeier, "Psalm 104 and the Hymn to Aten" (paper presented at the Annual Meeting of the Society of Biblical Literature, Nov. 21, 1998). Cf. Walton, pp. 163-165.

[22] To use another example, Egyptian creation myths told how the creator-god Ptah brought the world into being by words or his breath. He fashioned a giant air bubble in the cosmic ocean, separating the waters above from those below. Then he made land and all living things. Finished, he "rested," or was satisfied (R. T. Rundle Clark, *Myth and Symbolism in Ancient Egypt* [New York: Thames and Hudson, 1959], especially pp. 64, 65). The similarities with the Genesis Creation story does not mean that the biblical writer borrowed it

from the Egyptians, but that he made sure that he addressed specific points brought out in the Memphite theology since Israel would have encountered it during the people's sojourn in Egypt.

[23] Helmer Ringgren, *The Faith of the Psalmists* (Philadelphia: 1963), pp. 115, 116.

[24] Whybray, pp. 8, 9.

[25] Clifford, pp. 19-23.

[26] Sun Myung Lyu, "The Portrayal of the Righteous in the Book of Proverbs." Paper presented at the annual meeting of the Society of Biblical Literature, Nov. 21, 1999, Boston, Mass.

[27] And in ancient times its listeners, since most people did not know how to read and write and so would have had to hear the book recited.

[28] As we shall see later, "simple" implies a person with an as yet unformed character.

[29] Murphy, *Proverbs*, p. 4.

[30] See Lichtheim, Vol. I, pp. 73-76.

[31] We will explore the nature of the "fool" in chapter 5.

[32] Wisdom literature uses the Hebrew word to indicate young people still open to persuasion and not yet beyond all hope of rehabilitation (Whybray, p. 20).

[33] Some have suggested that this verse may allude to the way Egyptians portrayed *Maat*, goddess of truth and order, as holding symbols of life, riches, and order, but such imagery was so widespread and general in the ancient world that the biblical writer may well have picked it up from the surrounding culture without associating it with anything in particular. Wisdom in the Old Testament is not a goddess. Nowhere does anyone in the Bible speak to Wisdom, pray or make requests to her, or worship her.

[34] Extending from at least the time of the *Instruction of Ptahhotep*, the image of the true path and the false one—the two ways—has a long tradition as a metaphor to express moral teaching. Christ used it most dramatically in His sermon on the mount.

[35] Whybray, p. 50.

[36] Kidner, pp. 81, 82.

[37] Murphy, *Proverbs*, pp. 89, 90.

Chapter Two

THE PATH TO THE TRUSTWORTHY

A number of proverbs deal with the theme of trust. Trust, by the way, is whatever we owe our allegiance to. That in which we trust determines the shape of our lives and ultimately who we are. We base our decisions on what or whom we trust, and we reject anything connected to those things that we don't trust. Trust in and of itself is neutral, simply being part of human nature. Something inside each of us drives us to want to trust, to put our allegiance in the hands of some force outside us.[1] Scripture says that God planted the capacity to trust deep within our personalities, and as we shall see, the object of that trust should be God Himself.

But if we trust the wrong things, it can be disastrous. Wisdom will protect us from making bad choices as to what or whom to trust. As we saw in the previous chapter, wisdom is not abstract knowledge, but a relationship with the source of knowledge—God. He created the world, and even in its fallen state, He knows best how we should live in it. But if we reject true wisdom, we will put our trust in false gods. Such false gods do not have to be named Baal, Marduk, or Amon-Re. They can be family, nation, political philosophy, power, or wealth. The latter gods have captivated people in every age and culture.

Beware of Riches

The sages in the book of Proverbs have much to say about the folly of trusting in material wealth. Their warnings not to depend on wealth become especially significant when we remember that much of the biblical world regarded riches as a blessing from God and a sign of His favor. On the other hand, poverty indicated that the person had done something wrong and had fallen under a divine curse. Poverty or any misfortune was regarded as a divine punishment, as we see so dramatically argued in the book of Job.

Proverbs 23:4, 5 urges the reader not "to wear yourself out to get rich; be wise enough to desist. When your eyes light upon it, it is gone; for suddenly it takes wings to itself, flying like an eagle toward heaven." Our financial circumstances can change instantly. In the ancient world bandits, invading armies, drought, and disease could quickly wipe out wealth. Archaeologists sometimes find hoards of gold and silver or jewels buried in the floor of some ancient ruin. Did its owner try to hide it from invading armies? Did someone bury it to keep it safe, then die of disease or accident before he or she could recover it? Whatever the reason, the riches were lost forever to that person. Today stock market crashes, uncontrolled inflation, or other fickle factors of the economy can erase a bank balance or stock portfolio, sometimes within minutes.

The scribe compares vanishing riches to a startled bird that suddenly explodes into flight and disappears into the sky. It was an image that appealed to the Egyptian sages also. *The Instruction of Amenemope* warns against focusing on riches, especially if such wealth should come by theft. Stolen property will fly away into the sky like geese that vanish in a whir of wings.[2]

Proverbs 23:4, 5 cautions against the deceptiveness of riches. "They can become an all-consuming purpose in life, and also frustrating because they can disappear so easily."[3] But wisdom will enable the individual to see that "the unbridled pursuit of riches is senseless."[4] Without wisdom, though, those who chase wealth are trapped in an unending and hopeless quest.

Affluence may seem the best possible hedge against life's threats and vicissitudes. As the old joke goes, money may not buy happiness, but it pays for everything else. Thus most of us will feel tempted to do anything possible to accumulate financial reserves. We invest in stock or gold coins and try our luck at the lottery or local gambling casino—anything to get money. But Proverbs 11:4 cautions that "riches do not profit in the day of wrath."

We all recognize that life's disasters can wipe out even the best financial plans. But this passage has more in mind than just financial reversals. Roland Murphy sees "the day of wrath" going beyond normal catastrophes. "Implicitly, this is the Lord's wrath, and it cannot be bought off. Psalm 49 echoes the same teaching: 'you can't take it with you.' The riches of verse 4a are not the just desserts of the pious; there is the insinuation, especially in the context of verse 1a, that the riches have been preferred to 'justice' and something to be trusted in."[5] Assuming that wealth is God's automatic reward for good people is bad enough theology, as the book of Job reminds us, but to turn riches into a god is far worse.

Those who trust in their riches must face the fact that they are doomed (Prov. 11:28). But righteousness protects (verse 4). The sage compares the righteous to flourishing green leaves, a powerful symbol to a people living in a semiarid land dependent on often-capricious rainfall. The ancients might put their faith in land, gold, and herds, but they were no guarantee of safety.

We need to learn the same lesson. As much as we might be tempted to seek investments, stock portfolios, and other forms of assets to protect us from life's unending problems, it simply still doesn't work. Money will not shield us from disease, heartache, war, or—ultimately—death itself. And it must not be our god. For that we will have to answer to the God of heaven in the final judgment.

Violence Only Destroys

Some put their trust in raw power. Such power comes in many forms. It can be gangs, international mafia, political parties and philosophies, military power, the use of terror, or anything else we may employ to coerce and control others. Proverbs 3:31 advises us: "Do not envy the violent and do not choose any of their ways." The passage is a summary of Proverbs 1:1-19, which we will look at in greater detail.

The sage urges the readers ("my child" or "my son") not to give in to the temptation of easy riches dangled before them by violent criminals (verse 10). Although the imagery seems to be of banditry or thievery, the warning could apply to anything that uses force to gain wealth and power. Could it also apply to white-collar crime and get-rich schemes? Today thieves are just as likely to use computers and slick brochures as knives and guns.

But whatever kind of scheme we have in mind, crime is not just a modern problem. In the ancient world robbers lurked along deserted roads and the shadows of dry wadis. At night they hid outside a person's home, waiting for the householder to let his guard down so they could break in.[6] They could ambush their prey at any moment (verse 11). The criminal describes his deeds in the imagery of the Canaanite god of death, Mot, whose big jaws swallowed his victims (verse 12).[7] Promising all kinds of valuable loot, the criminal urges others to throw their lot in with him. The band of thieves would share and share alike (verses 13, 14).

But the wealth they seek is only a delusion. The biblical sage warns that violence and criminal activity will not lead to riches—only to self-destruction. Like trying to bait a fowler's net when the intended prey is watching, a life of crime will in the end fail (verse 17). "Criminals are less intelligent than birds, for they fail to see that they will be caught in the trap of their own violence."[8] Roland Murphy, taking a slightly different approach, suggests that the bird, while seeing the net, still foolishly flies into it, entrapping itself. The image thus alludes to the sheer folly of sinners.[9] However we interpret the imagery, the message is clear: greed destroys (verse 19).

Crime and violence are even more enticing today than in the biblical world. Many in the ancient world took up a life of crime as a means of survival. But today crime and even murder have become glamorous. All the media, especially television and the movies, glorify it, saturating the mind with graphic images of torture, death, and destruction. In the process, our consciences become desensitized. Video games make killing seem entertaining and harmless—until young people try it for real and find to their horror that the victim is truly dead and that the fantasy on the screen has horrible consequences in real life. War can also seem glamorous in the television news clips of videotapes from a precision laser-guided bombing run.

The constant depiction of violence convinces us that it is the answer to any problem. If only we could blow away our enemies as the characters in the movies or television programs do. But on the battlefield or in the shootouts in high schools, buddies die or are crippled for life. The only thing we can trust when it comes to violence is that it kills and destroys.

Propaganda and Other Big Lies

One of the most pervasive traits of human character is a willingness to lie. Satan introduced sin into the world with a lie, and human beings have been using falsehood ever since. We see it as a way to escape the consequences of our actions or as a means to get others to do our will. It is also a powerful and destructive weapon (Prov. 26:28). Lies can range from the simple denial of a child caught in a misdeed to corporations trying to win a multimillion-dollar lawsuit over false business practices or shoddy merchandise, to governments using propaganda to destroy enemies or cover up failed policies. Even Abraham, God's own chosen, tried to protect himself with a lie (Gen. 12:10-20).[10]

Many cultures honor a successful liar, and the ancient

Middle East was no exception. Ramses II (1279-1213 B.C.), after engaging the Hittites at the battle of Qadesh in 1274 B.C., announced a great victory over his foes. He inscribed his triumph on monuments throughout the land of Egypt. For 3,000 years historians believed him. Then archaeologists found the Hittite archives. In them the Hittites claimed that they had defeated the Egyptians. Most likely the battle was a draw since the two nations signed a peace treaty.[11] But Ramses II, as god on earth, son of Re the sun god, could not admit defeat. So he trusted in a big enough lie, and historians accepted it. He also ignored the advice of his own nation's sage who warned that the gods hated liars.[12] Today we listen as nations brag about how many enemy planes they shot down in the latest military engagement. Sometimes the total adds up to more than the other country had in its air force when the conflict began.

Whether it is Satan or some human dictator facing defeat, the temptation is to hide behind a big lie. Truth is always the first casualty of war or any other human misdeed. But persons (or institutions) that think they can lie their way out of any situation or use lies to gain their goals will find that truth will eventually destroy them. We must avoid such people. As the sage declares, "lying lips conceal hatred, and whoever utters slander is a fool" (Prov. 10:18). "An enemy dissembles in speaking while harboring deceit within" (Prov. 26:24).

The sage goes on to tell the reader to beware when an enemy speaks "graciously" (verse 25), because it conceals hatred (verse 26). But the God who keeps watch "on the evil and the good" (Prov. 15:3) will uncover all lies. Truth may, for example, come out in the public assembly in which citizens can challenge the official government version, the corporate public relations release and legal brief, the propaganda blitz—whatever big lie the enemy trusts in. The truth will eventually emerge, even if it takes 3,000 years. In the final judgment God will reveal all. Lies always destroy the liar in the end, for "whoever digs a pit will fall into it, and a stone will come back on the one who starts it rolling" (Prov. 26:27).[13] In fact, "it is better to be poor than a liar" (Prov. 19:22).

Those who try to build their lives on the use of lies also remind us of another thing the book of Proverbs tells us not to depend on: "Those who trust in their own wits are fools" (Prov. 28:26). Human beings have always been intrigued by those who try to do that. A character called the trickster has entered mythology all around the world. Native Americans enjoyed telling stories about a coyote that managed to talk or think his way out of all kinds of predicaments. Today we love to read about James Bond and other heroes who manage to escape the most impossible predicaments.

Even the Bible presents some individuals in ways that remind us of the trickster motif. Jacob and Samson lived by their wits. But it brought them much heartache and tragedy. Jacob thought he had outwitted his father-in-law, Laban, when breeding sheep. He assumed that he had accumulated his wealth through his own schemes. God had to remind him that it was not his own doing (Gen. 31:10-12). Sadly, his trickery passed on to his wives and sons, leading to more tragedy. Leah manipulated Rachel (Gen. 30:14-17), and Rachel deceived her father (Gen. 31:19-42). Finally Jacob's sons tricked him by selling Joseph into slavery.

As Murphy observes: "Wisdom is a gift of God (Prov. 2:6), but whoever claims to be wise is more foolish than the fool (Prov. 26:12; cf. Jer. 9:22-23)."[14] People who think they are wiser than anyone else wind up outwitting only themselves. But true wisdom will get us safely through life (Prov. 28:26). We can find wisdom on a human level by seeking the help of others (Prov. 13:20), men and women who are good role models and have learned from experience. But the ultimate source of wisdom is God. He is its originator, and we will never fail if we put our trust in Him (Prov. 28:25).

"Trust in the Lord with all your heart,"[15] and unlike the fool, who puts his faith in his wits, "do not rely on your own insight. In all your ways acknowledge him, and he will make straight your paths" (Prov. 3:5, 6). Ancient roads snaked around hills and other obstacles. Biblical engineers had no heavy road-building equipment to bulldoze away hills and fill in ravines. Nor could they bridge canyons and streams. In their minds only God had the ability to make roads straight. Today we might be able to blast through mountains and pave super-highways, but we recognize far more awesome challenges beyond our power.

Only Through the Help of God

As we saw in the previous chapter, wisdom comes from God. Whatever we accomplish in this life happens only through His aid. Thus the biblical sage counsels, "Commit your work to the Lord, and your plans will be established" (Prov. 16:3). "The human mind plans the way, but the Lord directs the steps" (verse 9). Although we may not recognize it in this life, whatever we accomplish is really the Lord's doing. He prepares the way for us, gives us the skills and insight to plan well, and many times He makes up for our deficiencies. Human science and technology have produced great wonders, but our minds are only feeble reflections of His creativity. We learn how to discover or do things only because He gave us minds and then guides us. Sometimes He takes us in surprising directions.

As Roland Murphy reminds us: "The final result is the Lord's doing, over which humans have no real control, and it may not be the 'success' that is yearned for. The poignant confession of Jeremiah 10:23 is appropriate here: 'I know, O Lord, that man's road is not his [to choose], that man, as he walks, cannot direct his own steps.'"[16] But when we get to God's destination, we would not have chosen otherwise.

Whatever may happen in life, we know that we can trust God. He alone is worthy of our absolute and unquestioning confidence. While He gives us great freedom, He desires that we seek His input instead of just doing what we think by ourselves is best. None of us can chart a wise course through life without trusting in divine wisdom (Prov. 20:27).

---

[1] We will look at one seeming exception: the person who puts confidence in his or her wits. But even the most self-centered person will at times let something or someone else make choices for him or her.

[2] Lichtheim, Vol. II, p. 152. The loss of wealth from thieves is always a danger in this life. But in an ultimate irony, the Egyptians, who tried to take their riches into the next life, found themselves the constant prey of tomb robbers.

[3] Roland E. Murphy, *Proverbs*, p. 175.

[4] *Ibid.*

[5] *Ibid.*, p. 81.

[6] Most moderns fail to grasp the message in such passages as Matthew 24:42-44; Luke 12:39, 40; 1 Thessalonians 5:2, 4; and 2 Peter 3:10. Unless we live in the inner city in the developed world, we think of crime as an occasional thing. But just as thieves lurked outside the biblical householder's home every night, so Christ could return at any time. We must always be alert.

[7] R.B.Y. Scott, *Proverbs/Ecclesiastes*, p. 38. Interestingly, Scripture also applies the imagery to the true God, who "will swallow up death forever" (Isa. 25:7).

[8] *Ibid.*, p. 39.

[9] Murphy, *Proverbs*, p. 10.

[10] Abraham called Sarah his sister since she was a half-sister. At best it was a half lie. But perhaps he was ironically and unconsciously telling more truth than he realized. Men and women in ancient Egyptian love poetry referred to their beloved as "my sister" and "my brother." See, for example, *Love Lyrics of Ancient Egypt*, trans. Barbara Hughes Fowler (Chapel Hill, N.C.: University of North Carolina Press, 1994), p. xiii.

[11] Ian Shaw and Paul Nicholson, *The Dictionary of Ancient Egypt* (New York: Harry N. Abrams, 1995), pp. 130, 131.

[12] See chapter 10 of *The Instruction of Amenemope* (Lichtheim, Vol. II, p. 154).

[13] The proverb is part of a discussion on lies and liars.

[14] Murphy, *Proverbs*, p. 21.

[15] The biblical symbol of the heart represents the whole personality. See *Dictionary of Biblical Imagery*, p. 368.

[16] Murphy, *Proverbs*, p. 121.

Chapter Three

THE PATH TO
CHARACTER AND REPUTATION

Modern Westerners, when they consider issues of character and personality, are most concerned with the individual and what makes each person unique. Wanting to develop our full potential to be totally "us," we fear being stereotyped or shoved into a common mold or a socially prescribed pattern. We may get upset if somebody wears the same dress or everybody drives a car just like ours. Children choose different careers and lifestyles than their parents. Intellectuals warn us about peer pressure and groupthink. Our desire is to stand out, to be different.

But the people of the biblical world were more interested in what individuals shared in common with their group than how they were different. Did they properly reflect the ways of their family, profession, village, tribe, or nation? People passed on the same traditions, ideas, and ways of doing things for centuries. Egyptian society remained basically identical for 3,000 years. Society in parts of the Mediterranean world even today still reflects many characteristics of Old Testament life. In such worlds people knew *who* they were because they knew *where* they belonged. Stereotyping, even if they understood the concept, would not have bothered them. After all, weren't you supposed to be like everyone else in your group?

Much like modern teenagers, the ancients found their identity in belonging to recognizable groups. Young people shape their identity and self-image through shared clothing and hairstyle, makeup, and slang. As they seek to clarify who they are, they first find identity by looking and dressing like everyone else their age. Teenagers today usually outgrow their strong group identity, but preindustrial societies maintained it. It provided security and stability in a dangerous and often chaotic world.

In the biblical world if you asked people who they were, they would reply that they were the son or daughter of So-and-so, living in such-and-such a village. In addition, they might be a wife, potter, farmer, or herder. Such facts told others who they were, and when you learned these facts you would have a good idea what these people were like. The members of each such group thought and lived much alike. The inhabitants of the Mediterranean world had what sociologists call collectivist personalities.[1]

Today we may joke about being able to spot a CPA or computer expert instantly in a crowd, but such people still lead widely varied lives. Even accountants have a wide range of interests and hobbies. We have great freedom—but often at great cost. Our individualistic perspective makes it harder for us to figure out who we are, and society has lost much of its cohesiveness. Both individuals and society as a whole have fragmented into isolated and often hostile pieces. People increasingly live by and for themselves.

"In contemporary North American culture we consider an individual's psychological makeup to be the key to understanding who he or she might be. We see each individual as bounded and unique, a more or less integrated motivational and cognitive universe, a dynamic center of awareness and judgment that is set over against other such individuals and interacts with them. This sort of individualism has been extremely rare in the world's cultures."[2]

Many moderns search hard and long to find the real "them." They don't want to be just extensions of their parents or reflections of a professional, gender, regional, or ethnic group. Sometimes they work so hard at being unique that they wind up being just like everyone else anyway—as we see, for example, when people wear clothing emblazoned with the same rock band or sports team, or when professionals drive the same expensive cars. But the biblical man or woman would demand, "What's wrong with being like everyone else in my family or trade?"

Most of the world has not worried about trying to express personal uniqueness. "In the Mediterranean world of antiquity such a view of the individual did not exist. There every person was embedded in others and had his or her identity only in relation to these others who formed a fundamental group. For most people this was the family, and it meant that individuals neither acted nor thought of themselves as persons independent of the family group. What one member of the family was, every member of the family was, psychologically as well as in every other way. Mediterraneans are what anthropologists call 'dyadic'; that is, they are 'other-oriented' people who depend on others to provide them with a sense of who they are."[3]

Although today we recognize that our individual uniqueness is special and must be preserved, since it reflects part of the image of God, the Bible just does not have much to say about it.[4] The world of Scripture was more interested in what people shared in common. The man and woman of the Bible would probably say we have gone overboard on the subject of individuality.

People in the Bible did not have family last names. (The use of a family name is a relatively recent innovation.) Instead, Scripture usually identifies a person as the son or daughter of someone else, or as born in a certain place. Thus the average individual thought of himself or herself as part of a family or place. Malina and Rohrbaugh point out that ancient society lumped all people belonging to a family as basically alike.[5]

What relevance does this have to our study of the Bible?

When we read Bible stories today we like to analyze the personalities of the various biblical individuals. Some have even tried to develop psychological theories and behavioral guidelines based on what they believe they see in the biographical material of the biblical text. They regard such stories as detailed insights on how to understand our own personalities. But this can be misleading or even dangerous, because "ancient people did not know each other very well in the way we think most important: psychologically or emotionally. They neither knew nor cared about psychological development and were not introspective. Our comments about the feelings and emotional states of characters in the biblical stories are simply anachronistic projections of our sensibilities on them. Their concern was how others thought of them (honor), not how they thought of themselves (guilt). Conscience was the accusing voice of others, not an interior voice of guilt (note Paul's comments in 1 Corinthians 4:1-4)."[6]

The Bible was more concerned about how people behaved than how they thought. Thus righteousness in Scripture, for example, involves more how God or a human being relates to others than some abstract quality inherent in a being. As we mentioned in chapter 1, righteous people are role models for other people to learn how to be righteous.

Too often we try to make biblical people act like illustrations from a modern psychology textbook or project into them our own often individualistic feelings and motivations. The biographical details and other material Scripture presents were intended to show right or wrong behavior and relationships, not psychological insights. They are examples of what is, or is not, righteousness. We must let the Scriptures and the biblical world interpret themselves. If we allow them to be a reflection of ourselves or of our modern world, we can run into problems.

For example, Martin Luther and commentators since his time have interpreted Paul by the Reformer's own angst-ridden personality rather than by reading the apostle in the context of his Mediterranean world. Just as we should not read modern

Western politics, business practices, literary theory, or anything else from the modern world back into Scripture, neither should we approach it from the perspective of how people think today. Human beings may remain basically the same throughout history, but each culture can greatly modify human behavior. The cultures of the biblical world were quite different from the world we live in today, and we must always keep this fundamental fact in mind or we will distort Scripture.

Modern psychological studies have taught us much about why we behave as we do today. But that does not mean we can automatically use it to interpret Scripture. To repeat, we must always remember that the Bible focuses on how people behaved and only in the most general sense on why they acted that way.

As we look at what the book of Proverbs has to say about human pride, we must approach it in the context of the group-oriented societies of the ancient world, not from the introspective perspective of modern society. We use psychology to analyze what emotional and reasoning processes motivate each action. But persons from the biblical world, if asked why they had done something, would, if they understood your question at all, have explained that they did something to gain honor or avoid shame—or simply that it was the proper thing to do.

Thus character and reputation in the Bible are revealed by behavior—especially toward others. Proud and arrogant people act one way toward others; humble people, another. Since arrogant and proud behavior usually hurts a group, the group will react negatively not out of a dislike for the abstract characteristic called pride itself, but because such actions have threatened the harmony or security of the group as a whole. The group—whether it be family, village, tribe, or race—was regarded as more important than a single person. People in such cultures see themselves primarily as members of their group and only secondarily as an individual. Each person views himself or herself through the eyes of the larger group. The ancients regarded themselves as threads composing the fabric of society. Moderns consider themselves complete universes in themselves.

As a result, our modern unrestrained individuality has broken down society's sense of unity. People find it harder to work together as teams. Rude and uncivil behavior has become rampant. Modern business is finding it increasingly difficult to locate employees with people skills. Western education has too often put the development of a child as an individual ahead of helping him or her to fit into groups and society as a whole. Sadly, conservative Christianity has at times encouraged this retreat into individualism, especially in its suspicion of education programs designed to help children cope with diversity. The group-orientation of the biblical world has much to teach us about how to get along with others. It can balance our individuality with a sense of community.

Things the Lord Hates

We see the group and external behavior orientation of the book of Proverbs when we look at such passages as Proverbs 6:16-19 and 16:5-7. As we examine these (and other) texts, notice how the biblical sage is more interested in the way people behave than what they are like psychologically. Psychological understandings are helpful, but they are not the types of categories the Bible uses. If we try to force them into our understanding of Scripture, we will distort its message.

Proverbs 6:16-19 is a numerical saying. Numerical sayings follow a formula that consists of giving a number and then exceeding it by one, as a point of emphasis (x; and x plus 1). It has a long history in the ancient Near East and appears a number of times in the Bible (for instance, Amos 1:3-2:8).[7] Also numerical sayings consist of a title line and a list of items or characteristics. The title line presents the feature(s) that the various items have in common.[8]

The title line of Proverbs 6:16-19 identifies the common characteristic of the items under consideration as things that God hates (verse 16). After stating that God dislikes six things and then raising the total by one to seven, the passage enumerates haughty eyes, a lying tongue, and hands that kill innocent people (verse 17); a heart (mind) that plans evil and feet that run about doing evil (verse 18);[9] perjury and anyone who causes dissension in the family (verse 19). All these things are an abomination to God (verse 16).[10] Notice that they are not internal psychological states but external, visible deeds. God hates certain ways we mistreat each other. By implication, if we do their opposite we will please God. He detests the way we get wrapped up in ourselves. We make ourselves, rather than God, the center of our world. But when we have concern and compassion for others, we reflect God's character and become more able to make Him central in our lives.

Bible writers saw external behavior as reflecting what a person inherently was. Good people do good things, and bad people perform bad deeds. They would not have conceived of people hiding behind psychological masks.[11] Today we see the relationship between psychological nature and deed as much more complex. Evil people can do good things for their own purposes or even from some part of their character not yet completely perverted. We see each individual as an intricate mosaic of good and bad motivations and traits. But even if we accept that, the relationship between what we do and what we are is still a powerful one. Modern psychology recognizes the illness and destructiveness of thinking one thing and doing another.

The "haughty eyes" of verse 17 have an echo in Proverbs 16:5, which also states that arrogance is an abomination (something detestable) to the Lord.[12] God is concerned about how His people treat each other. Verse 6 might seem at first glance to suggest that we can earn atonement through our own behavior.[13] But a more careful reading shows that is not the case.

The verb translated "atonement" "is primarily used in the Old Testament to denote the removal of sin through sacrifice. Here this is achieved not through sacrifice but by repentance: by a return to *faith* and *loyalty,* that is, to the standards of conduct characteristic of the relationship between Yahweh and Israel. This is put in another way in the second line: a man can be saved from the consequences of his evil deeds if the *fear of the LORD,* that is, his knowledge of what is due to God, still retains some power over him: reflection on this will enable him to *turn from evil* and so regain God's favour." [14]

Whybray adds that "this saying has no parallels in non-Israelite wisdom literature but expresses an Israelite point of view found also in the prophets and Psalms." [15] As we saw in the first chapter, a major difference between nonbiblical wisdom and that of Scripture is that the other wisdom documents taught that one could have success in life by what one did. The Bible teaches that true success comes from whom one worships.

Also, as we saw in chapter 1, the "fear of the Lord/God" is a fundamental and widespread image. It combines awe, reverence, faith, and obedience—the whole life of the believers as they relate to God. As His followers live out a concrete expression of their loyalty and faithfulness, they respond to the leading of God, who alone can provide atonement. A truly godly life can come only through God Himself.

Pride

We could summarize the seven things that God detests under a common heading: pride. The book of Proverbs has much to say about the specific subject of pride.

Pride precedes destruction (Prov. 16:18; cf. Prov. 18:12) and brings disgrace (Prov. 11:2). People filled with pride will reach beyond their capabilities, alienate others who will then turn against them, or trigger other events that will eventually bring shame and social disapproval. The ancients would have said that pride drives people to reject their station in life and reach for what was not rightfully theirs, that they sought more than was their due and so brought reproach upon their families. Both arrogance and pride are just plain sinful (Prov. 21:4). God cannot permit the proud to destroy society, and He will tear down their house (Prov. 15:25). "It is better to be of a lowly spirit among the poor than to divide the spoil with the proud" (Prov. 16:19). Pride destroys all positive human relationships, turning such persons against themselves (Prov. 8:36), others (Prov. 13:10), and God (Prov. 16:5).

Humility

The opposite of pride and arrogance is "the fear of the Lord" (Prov. 8:13), the first principle of true wisdom. The fear of the Lord leads to humility and brings wisdom (Prov. 11:2), riches, honor, and life (Prov. 22:4; 18:12). Humility is not some abstract and passive quality of the personality, but the totality of how we treat others—including God. In the Old Testament, humility meant living out the principles of the fear of the Lord. The New Testament expands our understanding of humility. Christ came to show in His life on earth that true humility is serving others just as He took upon Himself the humility of a servant to serve and save us (Phil. 2:1-8).

A Good Name

Proverbs 22:1 states that "a good name is to be chosen rather than great riches." In the eyes of the biblical world a name symbolized what we would today call a person's reputation. Reputation involved more than just what others thought of a person. It contained all that he or she was. All that an individual was—aside from the social status one was born into—derived from what she or he had done. Both reputation and what we would today call character consisted of how a person treated others and fit into his or her place in society.

Character and reputation were not personal traits or abilities but how the individual lived. And the most important part of living was what one did in relationship to others. People had a good reputation not for having some special skills or intelligence, but whether they honored their parents, took care of the widows and orphans, and were humble before God.

The wisdom literature of Egypt and Mesopotamia was the ancient counterpart of today's books on how to succeed in business, politics, and society. Follow these rules, they said, and you will impress others and acquire the honor, wealth, and power appropriate to your position in life. It didn't matter what you really were as long as you did the socially approved thing. In contemporary society we have added image consultants and public relations experts. They can create a favorable public image for anyone with enough money and turn even disasters into assets. But the biblical sages would not have understood the world of sound bites, spin doctors, media campaigns, and image creation. How has one lived? That was the important thing to the men and women of the Bible. Lifestyle was not something that could be changed by a public relations consultant arranging the right media exposure. From a biblical perspective, how we live in relation to others constitutes the very core of our being.

In the honor/shame societies[16] of the biblical world reputation meant everything. Reputation was what others thought you were. "The way others perceive a person is equivalent to a person's (or family's) actual social worth."[17] The goal was to convince society that you were representative of your group whether you really were or not. The nonbiblical wisdom tradition taught that if you followed its teachings people would assume that you were the kind of person you wanted to be—that you were a worthy and typical scribe, courtier, landowner, or whatever. By following the cosmic order you could impress society and avoid social blunders.

But the Israelite wisdom writings began to shift that perspective. You could acquire a good reputation only by actually becoming a good person. What you did was not a social pose, but actually stemmed from the good motives now driving you—motives resulting from your fear of the Lord. As we would phrase it today, it was not *creating* an image, but actually *becoming* that kind of person.

More important than what people think we are is what kind

of people we actually are in our true inner nature. But even more profound—and subtle—Proverbs continues the biblical transformation of reputation from being what we humans think we are to what God perceives us as. The only important thing will eventually become not how society views us, but what God sees. The New Testament teaches that the ultimate reputation is the Father seeing Christ in each believer. The only important reputation is how God regards His human children.

If we live in the fear of the Lord and the recognition that we are His sons and daughters, we will treat others as He does and will come to reflect His character. All our actions and deeds will be expressions of love and concern for others, the opposite of pride and arrogance, which focus only on self.

Many today express concern over a lack of character education in the public school systems. Character education teaches young people skills in getting along with other people. But we need more than just the ability to interact successfully with others. We must be more than just civil and courteous. We must genuinely love each other. Do we show respect to others because they are fellow sons and daughters of God—or is it only a technique to impress, a way of being politically correct? Do we honor those around us for who they are—or just to get ahead in life? According to Scripture only true wisdom—the fear of the Lord—can lead to the love Christ displayed in His life and that He calls for us to exhibit in our own.

God created us to love and care for each other in ways that echo the love among the members of the Godhead. True wisdom means acquiring through God's Spirit a character and reputation that reflect our Creator. Our name must uphold His name.

---

[1] For a convenient summary of some of the differences between the collectivist and the individualistic personality, see the chart on page 164 of Bruce J. Malina and Richard L. Rohrbaugh, *Social-Science Commentary on the Gospel of John* (Minneapolis: Fortress Press, 1998).

[2] Bruce J. Malina and Richard L. Rohrbaugh, *Social-Science Commentary*

on the Synoptic Gospels (Minneapolis: Fortress Press, 1992), p. 113. Although Malina and Rohrbaugh are writing about the New Testament period, the Mediterranean world had changed little from Old Testament times, and even today many of the patterns they describe still linger, especially in rural areas.

[3] Ibid.

[4] I have discussed the sacredness of our individuality elsewhere. See Gerald Wheeler, Beyond Life: What the Bible Has to Say About Life, Death, and Immortality, pp. 12. 13.

[5] Malina and Rohrbaugh, Social-Science Commentary on the Synoptic Gospels, p. 113.

[6] Ibid.

[7] Roland E. Murphy, Wisdom Literature and Psalms (Nashville: Abingdon Press, 1983), p. 74. Cf. R. N. Whybray, The Book of Proverbs, pp. 39, 40; R.B.Y. Scott, Proverbs/Ecclesiastes, p. 59.

[8] Roland E. Murphy, Wisdom Literature: Job, Proverbs, Ruth, Canticles, Ecclesiastes, and Esther (Grand Rapids: Eerdmans, 1981), Vol. XIII, p. 180.

[9] Feet were the biblical symbol for the active part of the personality. The Mediterranean world divided the human personality into three aspects, or zones. Hands, feet, fingers, and legs often stood for behavior and deeds or that part of the personality which interacted with the external world. See Malina and Rohrbaugh, Social-Science Commentary on the Synoptic Gospels, pp. 55, 56.

[10] The Egyptian Instruction of Amenemope also regarded moral offenses such as lying as something the gods abhorred (Miriam Lichtheim, Ancient Egyptian Literature, Vol. II, p. 154).

[11] Jesus constantly attacked the Pharisees as hypocrites, from the Greek term for actor or playing a part. But even here the criticism reflects the Mediterranean concept of an inseparable linkage between what a person was and his or her behavior. The hypocrite's behavior did not represent the person's true nature, not because of hidden psychological depths, but because of simple deception.

[12] To a great extent the ancients would have considered arrogance as trying to rise above one's station in life. Moderns would see it more as feeling too superior in a world of equals.

[13] The New Revised Standard Version says that loyalty and faithfulness atone for iniquity. By implication, such faithfulness would be to the God of Israel.

[14] Whybray, p. 94.

[15] Ibid.

[16] For an understanding of how honor and shame drove biblical society, see Malina and Rohrbaugh, Social-Science Commentary on the Synoptic Gospels, pp. 76, 77, 213, 214, 309-311, and Social-Science Commentary on the Gospel of John, pp. 121-124.

[17] Malina and Rohrbaugh, Gospel of John, p. 124.

Chapter Four

THE PATH TO SOCIAL HEALING

Today modern medicine has increasingly recognized that health involves far more than the body. It includes the emotions and social relationships. A whole family or even an entire society can become ill just as an individual can. Medicine and psychology now realize that physical disease can have emotional causes, that emotions can trigger physical symptoms, and that we have to treat the whole person.

The same principles apply to families and other groups. Groups can become ill from either physical or emotional factors. Malnutrition and endemic infection can plague communities and societies. Stress and damaged personal relationships can affect both physical and emotional health. In addition, groups struggle with illnesses caused by alienation and unhealthy relationships. Such illnesses are as real as infections and cancers. And they can be equally as fatal if ignored. Families and societies can die as well as individuals.

Just as we have come to recognize that we must treat the whole individual to have full healing, so we have to deal with whole families, workforces, or other groups. In order to heal one member of a family or society, we may have to deal with the whole family or community. Healing must touch all that a person or group is. Beyond that, we must examine any external factors outside the group that may be affecting it and deal with these factors in a manner similar to the way we would eliminate any environmental factors that might make the individual sick.

The biblical world held a similar concept. For example, they seemed to sense that social strife can be just as much a symptom of social illness as a fever or headache is of a biological one. Or that a family with estranged members needs healing. When David exiled his son Absalom, it aggravated an already sick[1] family. Joab, recognizing the unhealthy circumstances, tried to heal the situation (2 Sam. 14). Although the people of the Bible did not know much about biological disease, they did have remarkable insights into dealing with social illness. The Bible can teach us much about the latter.

Malina and Rohrbaugh comment that "in the contemporary world we view disease as a malfunction of the organism which can be remedied, assuming cause and cure are known, by proper biomedical treatment. We focus on restoring a sick person's ability to function, to do. Yet often overlooked is the fact that health and sickness are always culturally defined and that in other societies the ability to function is not the heart of the matter. In the ancient Mediterranean, one's state of being was more important than one's ability to act or to function. The healers of that world focused on restoring a person to a valued state of being rather than an ability to function."[2] Today's men and women drive themselves to accomplish great things, but find themselves unhappy and lacking any sense of self-worth.

Modern medicine may be able to do wonders with physical problems, but it cannot restore a person's self-image or social acceptance. New treatments have stopped cancers, but society has been struggling to know how to relate to such patients as human beings. Family, friends, and coworkers have no idea how to relate to them. Are they still sick or well? Is it safe for them to return to work? Will the cancer return? Do you or don't you discuss what they have gone through? Radiation and drugs may arrest the disease, but they cannot erase the patient's and family's continuing fears and uncomfortable feelings toward the cancer survivor. Patients may be physically well, but we are not sure how to return them to their former place in society.

Surgery may be able to relieve much of the physical crippling and scarring of accidents, but it cannot treat the emotional and psychological trauma and scarring of the event itself. A person may be able to get a drug addiction under control, but what about all that the person did to family and others while trapped in the addiction? Who will heal broken relationships?

Jesus' healing ministry particularly concentrated on returning persons to society. After healing a blind man's sight or removing the physical ravages of leprosy, He restored them to the society that had considered them social outcasts. In the words of Malina and Rohrbaugh, He would remove the biological malfunction, then deal with the social illness, the state of being. When healing leprosy, He would tell the victims to go see the priests at the Temple. The priests had diagnosed their physical condition, then classified and quarantined them as social outcasts. Only the priests could readmit into society. The most vital part of that restoration was dealing with the person's sin problem. Sin afflicted the whole person—body, emotions, and social relations—so the whole person would not be considered healed until the sin was removed and the individual brought back to society and God.

"Anthropologists thus distinguish between *disease*—a biological malfunction affecting an organism—and *illness*—a disvalued state of being affecting a person in which social networks have been disrupted and meaning lost. Illness is not so much a biomedical matter as it is a social one. It is attributed to social, not physical causes. Because sin is a breach of interpersonal relationships, sin and sickness go together. Illness is not so much a medical matter as a matter of deviance from cultural norms and values."[3] In keeping with those terms, the world today suffers far more from *illness* than it does *disease*.

Elsewhere Malina and Rohrbaugh observe that "in non-

Western medicine, the main problem with sickness is the experience of the sick person being dislodged from his/her social moorings and social standing. Social interaction with family members, friends, neighbors, and village mates comes to a halt. To be healed is to be restored to one's social network."[4]

It is here that medicine still fails—and always will by itself—and where the church has much to offer. The church can lead persons to God's forgiveness of guilt and bring them back into community. If the old community refuses to accept victims of social illness, the church can replace it with the new community of Christ. Church members become brothers and sisters, social mates, all interwoven into a new social network with Christ as its head. The church can give them back the state of being that they had lost through sin and social illness.

Agents of Social Illness

The book of Proverbs deals with the kind of illness we have been looking at in two ways. First, it tells us what to avoid so that we will not become sicker. Second, it points out what we should do to regain our health in the biblical sense of our whole being, especially emotionally and spiritually.[5]

The biblical sages constantly and emphatically warned their readers against the way of the wicked, a primary cause of social and spiritual illness. "Do not enter the path of the wicked, and do not walk[6] in the way of evildoers. Avoid it; do not go on it; turn away from it and pass on" (Prov. 4:14, 15). Just as a wrong lifestyle can lead to physical illness, so a wrong lifestyle ("walking in the way of the wicked") can cause social and spiritual illness.

Certain kinds of people will infect others with their own particular social/spiritual illness in a manner similar to those who carry biological illnesses. They need to be isolated or they will disrupt the community and cause spiritual death. "Leave the presence of a fool, for there you do not find words of knowledge. It is the wisdom of the clever to understand where they go, but the folly of fools misleads" (Prov. 14:7, 8). As we shall see in chapter 5, a "fool" in the wisdom writings is not someone mentally deficient, but a person who deliberately rebels against God and the rules of life. They can be quite intelligent, but they use their minds to go against the way of the universe and seek to lead others to follow their example.

The Hebrew word that English translations render as "way" in the book of Proverbs has the sense of "conduct." Proverbs 14:7, 8 "makes moral reflection the essence of shrewdness, whereas we tend to reduce shrewdness to business-sense. Likewise the essence of folly is mental dishonesty: not merely falling short of the truth (as we must), but side-stepping it."[7] Verse 8 not only describes folly as deception, but also identifies it as such.[8]

The book of Proverbs lists many of the carriers of social/spiritual illness. We touch upon some of them throughout this book, but they include scoffers, gossipers, troublemakers, liars, perjurers, the lazy, those with violent tempers, and so forth. Often Proverbs classifies them under the general category of fools, though the Hebrew text has specific words for each kind of fool.

Proverbs 16:27-30 lists some of the things that the socially ill do to spread their condition. They concoct evil or mischief, and their rumors or tales burn others (verse 27). Perverse individuals[9] spread[10] strife, and their whispering campaigns turn even close friends against each other (verse 28). The violent seduce their neighbors into all kinds of socially disruptive trouble (verse 29). Sometimes the wicked don't even have to speak to cause social turmoil. They can stir up mischief without uttering a word. Subtle innuendos can plant seeds of suspicion and hostility (verse 30). Politics is especially skilled at this today through its use of political cartoons and other media.

Proverbs 6:12-14 paints a similar picture of the subtle and insidious evil that a "fool" can use to tear a group or society apart without saying a word or making a direct accusation. Today the wicked can fake photographs or other evidence to destroy those they hate, but the ancients could do it with just a few gestures.

Proverbs 22:24, 25 describes another infectious agent lurking in human society: those controlled by anger or ready to explode at the slightest provocation.[11] Such people can incite mobs or start vendettas. To associate with them may mean winding up like them (verse 25).

We find in Proverbs 23:6-8 more types of people to avoid lest they spread social illness. The "stingy" would be especially disruptive in a society that barely managed to exist only by sharing the scarce resources of a harsh environment, but modern society has almost institutionalized greed. Consider, for example, how advertising and business depend on people wanting the latest and newest product.

The stingy people that the sage has in mind here encourage you to share, but they don't practice their own advice. The behavior of such hypocrites is so nauseating they will cause you to gag, perhaps like a hair tickling your throat (verse 7), and anything you say to them is only wasted breath (verse 8).

Roland Murphy notes that the vomiting mentioned in verse 8 and the pleasant words the guest offers to the stingy host came from the same mouth. Suggesting that we should take the vomiting as only metaphorical, Murphy sees the guest as "disgusted at his own words because they have been proven untrue, or unworthy of the occasion."[12]

Perhaps we might find modern counterparts to the stingy mentioned by the sage among those wealthy individuals who actively spearhead fund-raising drives but always seem to find ways not to donate themselves. Sometimes they even profit by charging their services and personal expenses to the charitable campaign. The sage also advises the reader not to counsel such fools. They will only despise you for your efforts (verse 9). "Fools may not be failing in real intelligence, but they just will not 'listen' or take to heart any advice."[13]

Breaking Social Covenants

Next we turn to imagery that we previously looked at in another context. The early chapters of Proverbs use the figure of the adulterous woman to warn against being seduced by false wisdom. But the power of the imagery is that it also depicts a literal situation and problem. We understand the allusions to a loose woman because we encounter them in real life. Good imagery or metaphors can communicate simultaneously on more than one level at a time. The Bible can teach on several levels through the same illustration.[14] When Proverbs compares false wisdom to an adulterous woman, we instantly recognize many of the snares of deceptive wisdom. And at the same time the sage reminds us of the very real problems that extramarital affairs cause in human society.

If we consider the imagery of the adulterous woman from a literal perspective, it forces us to recognize that sex is a powerful social force. Otherwise the biblical writer would not have used it to portray graphically the dangers of false wisdom. As we shall see later, when properly employed in the confines of marriage, sex can help bind a couple together for life. But when released outside of marriage, it can rip the social fabric to shreds.

Thus several sections of the book of Proverbs look at the danger of impurity and infidelity through the illustration of the loose woman or harlot. They include Proverbs 2:16-19, 5:1-23, 6:23-35, and 7:4-27. All these passages stress the lure[15] of unrestrained and inappropriate sexuality and the inevitable destruction it can cause both to the individual and to his or her relationships with the family and larger community. The loose woman (remember that this is largely a male-oriented society that produced the book of Proverbs) "forsakes the partner of her youth and forgets her sacred covenant" (Prov. 2:17; cf. Prov. 7:19). She has forgotten not only her bond and promise to her spouse, but also the God who created the marriage covenant. Thus by implication she has also abandoned God Himself. Covenant is an image that later Bible writers used not only of the relationship between husband and wife (Mal. 2:14), but also that between Israel and its God.

Such behavior leads to death (Prov. 2:18; 7:27). Whybray comments that death is not necessarily an exaggeration or a metaphor because Leviticus 20:10 states that death was the penalty for adultery. Proverbs 5:9-14 calls for Israel to exclude adulterers from the community, which could also lead to death because the offender would no longer have society's support and protection.[16] The offended spouse and family could also start a blood feud with the adulterer's family.

Today sexually transmitted diseases kill millions. HIV has particularly devastated Africa, India, and Southeast Asia, wiping out whole generations. But that is not the only problem, bad as it may be. Adultery also destroys character and reputation (Prov. 5:14). "The primary thought of these verses [Proverbs 5:9-14] is not that loose living invites disease (though 11 may well include this), but that it dissipates irrevocably the powers a man has been given to invest. He will wake up to find that he has been exploited by his chosen circle, with whom he had no real ties (9, 10), condemned by his conscience (11-13), and on the brink of public ruin (14)."[17] Sexually immoral relationships made people outcasts in the biblical world's closely-knit culture, outcasts who could only destabilize and demoralize society.

Thus the greatest damage caused by adultery is what it does to people themselves and their relationships with others. All experience a loss of trust. Even the adulterer is no longer sure what he or she will or will not do. Covenants and family honor have been betrayed. Above all else, adultery leads to spiritual death.[18] Proverbs 5:3-8 draws a sharp contrast "between the delectable promises held out by the adulteress and the terrible fate which befalls those who listen to her."[19]

The sage shakes his head over the whole idea of an extramarital affair. Proverbs 6:30-35 observes that people understand why thieves will steal because of hunger. Few will despise them even if they get caught and as punishment have to pay sevenfold and forfeit their household goods. After all, they were desperate. "But he who commits adultery has no sense; he who does it destroys himself. He will get wounds and dishonor,[20] and his disgrace will not be wiped away" (verses 32, 33). In addition, he has to face the wife's brothers or husband whose honor the adulterer has sullied (verses 34, 35).[21]

The biblical sage knew what is even more obvious in modern society—sex is powerfully tempting. It makes a wonderful commodity to sell, as almost every movie, television program, and media ad reminds us. But when flaunted outside of marriage, it destroys. Marriage, and every trusting relationship it touches, shatter. Adultery and the pursuit of sex outside marriage lead to children either abandoned or tossed from parent to parent. Children lose not only their security but also vital role models. They grow up knowing only broken relationships, and it is likely that they will replicate them in their own lives.

The typical Western classroom today is lucky to have more than a fraction of its students still living with both of their parents. A survey in the United States revealed that the number of families with both parents present dropped from 73 percent in 1972 to only 51.7 percent in 1998. During that same period of time, single parent homes rose from 4.7 percent to 18.2 percent, and homes with unmarried parents increased from 4.7 percent to 9.2 percent.[22] Blended families of divorced and remarried parents also jumped. Parallel or even greater increases appear in other parts of the world.

Teachers can see the hurt and anger in their student bodies. These young people will grow up handicapped and more vulnerable to marital breakup or dysfunction. Recent studies indicate that more and more children of divorce do not marry at all.

Society has paid a terrible price as a result of the breakdown of marriage. Even those who protest the trend are not immune from it. Too many conservative public figures in the United States have challenged the adulterous affairs of others, only to have their own immorality later exposed.

Sex outside of marriage has been one of the most destructive and infectious agents of social illness.[23] But society can be both inoculated against it and healed of it. As we shall see when we look at what Proverbs has to say about marriage in chapter 12, the biblical sage urges his readers to commit themselves to their marriage partners (for example, Prov. 5:18, 19). "Why should you be intoxicated, my son, by another woman and embrace the bosom of an adulteress?" (verse 20). Social decay screams at us that we need strong and faithful marriages. It's for our own best interests—as well as those of society at large—to keep our covenants with our spouses.

But there is still another reason. "For human ways are under the eyes of the Lord, and he examines all their paths" (verse 21). God is watching, and those who profess to be loyal to Him must answer for what they do. "The arguments of common sense are undergirded by appeal to Yahweh's judgment and the inner contradictions of sin."[24]

Alcoholism

A major cause of social illness in the ancient world was one that is an even greater plague in modern society: alcoholism. "Wine is a mocker," the sage declares, "strong drink[25] a brawler, and whoever is led astray by it is not wise" (Prov. 20:1). Wine drinking was common in the ancient world. In Egypt bread and beer, or fermented grain mash, were two of the main foods.[26]

Wine, however, can reach only a certain percentage of alcohol before the fermentation process stops. The ancient world did not have high alcoholic-content distilled products as the modern world does. Also, the Greeks and Romans routinely diluted the wine with water as a matter of course, as apparently did the Jews (see, for example, Isa. 1:22; 2 Macc. 15:39). For the Greeks the normal mixture was three parts water to one part wine.[27] Other ratios of water to wine included two to one, four to one, and five to two.[28] The alcohol would kill some of the microorganisms in the often-polluted water, perhaps the reason the apostle Paul advised Timothy to drink some wine (1 Tim. 5:23). The wine would likely have reduced the level of microorganisms upsetting the younger man's intestinal tract. The Greeks frowned on those who drank undiluted wine, considering them barbarians.[29]

Wine and ancient beer might have had a low alcohol content, but it was still possible to get drunk if one consumed enough. Many must have drunk to escape the poverty and hard life of the typical Israelite peasant (Prov. 31:6). The wealthy would have had even more opportunity to indulge. Whatever the reason, the sage warns of the dangers of alcohol. It could lead to poverty (Prov. 21:17;[30] 23:21).

Alcohol could be especially threatening to social order when consumed by leadership. Among other problems, inebriated leaders could forget what they had decreed or pervert the rights of the oppressed while under the influence of alcohol (Prov. 31:4, 5). This would be a greater problem in a limited literate society in which laws were not printed or easily available. Nor did ancient governments have as many checks and balances as in a modern constitutional system.

R. N. Whybray reminds us that, contrary to popular assumptions, ancient Near Eastern kings were not above the law. He cites the Egyptian instructional text by Merikare in which the king tells his son, "Do justice while you are on earth; . . . do not oppress the widow; supplant no man in the property of his father; . . . be on your guard against punishing unjustly.' Nevertheless the king's position gave him opportunities to *twist* or break *the law*. The Babylonian *Advice to a Prince* gives an impressive catalogue of acts of injustice which the king is liable to commit, together with a list of the corresponding acts of divine retribution which will follow."[31] An alcoholic ruler would be more likely to pervert justice to his or his friends' own ends.

The stories of King Ahasuerus and his wife Vashti (Esther 1:10-22) and Herod's execution of John the Baptist illustrate what could happen when drinking affected a ruler's reasoning power. At the very least alcohol could bring governmental operations to a halt.

The sage gives a sharply drawn picture of the effects of alcohol in Proverbs 23:29-35. Whybray calls the passage "a vivid portrait of the drunkard, based on acute observation and psychological insight. . . . Such passages show that some wisdom teachers were sufficiently skilled to break away from the traditional form of the short saying and make effective use of their imagination. Such longer passages are characteristic of the Egyptian Instruction." [32]

The book of Proverbs depicts alcohol as biting like a serpent (verse 32; cf. Deut. 32:33) and leading to hallucinations (verse 33). But despite all the problems alcohol causes, its victim will not give up drinking (verse 35). Derek Kidner regards the passage as "an unforgettable study of the drunkard, as he is seen (29) and as he sees (33-35). His imagination is as uncontrollable as his legs (34); and if there is pathos in his first fascination (31), there is far more in his final bravado (35)." [33]

The Talmud, which is a rabbinical commentary on the scriptural law, indicates that those who have drunk one cup of wine are like lambs. Those who have imbibed two cups of wine resemble lions. After three cups of wine, persons act like apes. By the time they have guzzled down four cups of wine, they behave like pigs. [34]

Modern humanity finds itself in the same trap as its ancient counterparts, only worse, as the easy availability of distilled and more powerful alcoholic beverages has compounded the problem. Alcoholism is one of the most insidious social ills stalking the modern world. It causes death by traffic accident, leads to violence, and triggers all kinds of physical illnesses as well as emotional and psychological ones. Drinking impairs the judgment and costs businesses and governments millions of dollars in lost productivity. Many governments have attempted to fight the rampant alcoholism in their nations, but often find themselves addicted to the profits and taxes from the beverage industry.

Alcoholic parents create dysfunctional families as drinking distorts and destroys all kinds of social relationships. Pregnant mothers who drink can physically impair their unborn children. The addiction to alcohol both makes the alcoholic a social outcast and damages the fabric of society as a whole.

Avoiding Social Illness

God in His power can heal the social illness caused by adultery, unrestricted sex, and alcoholism. He can restore its victims to society. But how much better it would have been not to have become infected in the first place.

Proverbs 16:17 declares that "the highway of the upright avoids evil; those who guard their way preserve their lives."[35] Avoiding evil makes for a smoother passage through life.

"The teaching of the wise is a fountain of life, so that one may avoid the snares of death" (Prov. 13:14). Just as finding a reliable source of water in an arid land protects life, so will accepting the counsel of the wise.

The ancients used snares to catch wild birds and small game. Hunters put them along favorite animal trails or spread food in front of the trap to attract the unsuspecting creatures. But those who listen to the wise will not be deceived by such trickery. They will be able to spot the traps and dangers along the path of life. And the life that wisdom offers is not just a protection against death but a quality of life that only God can give.

"The wise are cautious and turn away from evil, but the fool throws off restraint and is careless" (Prov. 14:16). We all have known people who seem driven to take risks. They might be quite brilliant in many ways, but from the perspective of the book of Proverbs they are fools because they refuse to accept wisdom. Such individuals do not want to conform to the way God created life and the universe to function. Risk-taking fools can be quite charming and convincing. But we should not associate with those who rebel against wisdom (Prov. 14:7).

Wisdom teaches us where we should be going in life, whereas the fool will only get us sidetracked into folly (verse 8).

As we see throughout the book of Proverbs, the sages want us to find wisdom and avoid folly. Wisdom is a God-given understanding of God Himself and the way He wants us to live, while folly is rebellion against and rejection of the divine path of life. The second chapter of Proverbs[36] outlines the value of such wisdom. The chapter describes wisdom as something that we can obtain only after great effort (Prov. 2:1-5), is God-given (verses 6-9), and is a moral safeguard (verses 10-22). The passage constantly uses the metaphor of "path" or "way." Verses 16-19 warn against false wisdom. (We earlier looked at this same passage on a less metaphorical level when we examined the social problem of marital infidelity.)

To find true wisdom calls for a search as hard and long as we might expend for hidden treasure (verse 4). The difficulty we have in finding wisdom is not God's fault, but a result of our finite and fallen nature. When we reach the point that God can give us wisdom (verse 6), it will shield those who walk blamelessly (verse 7), guard justice, and protect His followers (verse 8). It protects justice because it enables us to understand what true justice is (verse 9). As wisdom comes into us (the heart in verse 10 is the reasoning part of the personality) we will avoid the kind of problems that folly, or rebellion, would lead us into (verse 12). We will see through the deceptions practiced by the fools and unrighteous and will cease associating with them (verses 12-15), especially the false wisdom of the "loose woman," or as Roland Murphy likes to call her, "Dame Folly."

In conclusion, the sage urges all to "walk in the way of the good, and keep to the paths of the just" (verse 20). The righteous will thrive in the land God has given them (verse 21), but the wicked will perish like plants pulled by the roots and thus cut off from the land (verse 22).

Although some have observed that the book of Proverbs does not advocate exactly the same kind of Israelite lifestyle that the Pentateuch delineates,[37] the phrase "cut off from the land" alludes to the teachings of the books of Moses (cf. Deut. 28:63). Proverbs speaks in principles that fit any kind of culture or life situation, including our postindustrial world with its societies often very different from those of the biblical world.

---

[1] Today we would use the term *dysfunctional.*

[2] Bruce J. Malina and Richard L. Rohrbaugh, *Social-Science Commentary on the Synoptic Gospels,* pp. 70, 71.

[3] *Ibid.,* p. 71.

[4] ———, *Social-Science Commentary on the Gospel of John,* pp. 113, 114.

[5] The plan of salvation, though fundamental to spiritual healing and health, will not be explored in detail here.

[6] The imagery of walking was a fundamental metaphor for the way a person lived, either for good or bad, and appears in both the Old and New Testaments. Paul, as a concordance will quickly reveal, used it as his way of emphasizing how we should live according to God's will.

[7] Derek Kidner, *Proverbs,* p. 107.

[8] Roland E. Murphy, *Proverbs,* p. 104.

[9] Literally, the person who turns things upside down (*ibid.,* p. 124).

[10] It is the same word used of Samson's release of the flaming foxes or jackals to destroy the Philistine grain fields in Judges 15:5 (Kidner, p. 122).

[11] The passage echoes chapter 9 of *The Instruction of Amenemope.* See Miriam Lichtheim, *Ancient Egyptian Literature,* Vol. II, pp. 153, 154. This section of the book of Proverbs has many parallels to the Egyptian wisdom documents. R. N. Whybray outlines the correspondences. See R. N. Whybray, *The Book of Proverbs,* pp. 132-141.

[12] Murphy, p. 175.

[13] *Ibid.*

[14] Great literature often speaks on more than one level at a time, and the Bible exploits this opportunity whenever possible. One of the dangers of paraphrased versions of the Bible is that in the translators' desire to be clear, they remove the biblical writer's deliberate ambiguity and focus only on one level of meaning. In the process they eliminate the other levels that the author may have intended.

[15] The honey dripping from the lips of the loose woman (Prov. 5:3) is sweet at first, but leaves a bad aftertaste (Kidner, p. 69).

[16] Whybray, p. 23.

[17] Kidner, p. 70.

[18] Murphy, *Proverbs,* p. 16.

[19] Whybray, p. 36.

[20] The worst possible punishment in an honor/shame society.

[21] In biblical society stronger emotional ties existed between brothers and

sisters than between husbands and wives (Malina and Rohrbaugh, p. 88). We see this close brother/sister bond in operation in the story of the rape of Tamar (2 Sam. 13). Tamar and Absalom were full brother and sister while she and Ammon were only half brother and sister. The same dynamic is at work in the story of the rape of Dinah (Gen. 34).

[22] Peter Jensen, "The Changing Family," Baltimore *Sun*, Jan. 2, 2000.

[23] Israelite sages were not the only ones to fear unrestrained sexuality. Even the more permissive society of ancient Egypt worried about it. For example, the New Kingdom scribe Any expressed concern about the impact a visiting woman could have on a community. "Beware of the woman who is a stranger in your town. Do not stare at her as she goes by, and avoid sexual intercourse with her. Such a woman, away from her husband, is like deep water whose depth is unknown" (Cited in Joyce Tyldesley, *Daughters of Isis*, p. 179). Compare this with Proverbs' caution about the "strange" or "foreign" woman.

[24] Kidner, p. 71.

[25] Some translators render the Hebrew word *shekar* as "beer." The Talmud defines strong drink as undiluted wine (Robert H. Stein, "Wine-Drinking in New Testament Times," *Christianity Today*, June 20, 1975, p. 10). Other scholars regard *shekar* as referring to any alcoholic drink other than grape wine. Wine could also be made from pomegranates, dates, honey, raisins, barley, and apples (*International Standard Bible Encyclopedia*, vol. 1, p. 993).

[26] Hilary Wilson, *Egyptian Food and Drink* (Aylesbury, Eng.: Shire Publications, 1988), p. 7.

[27] *International Standard Bible Encyclopedia*, vol. 4, p. 1070.

[28] Stein, p. 9. It has been suggested that Jesus had the wine jars at the wedding of Cana first filled with water because people expected it to be diluted anyway.

[29] *Ibid.*, p. 10.

[30] Besides an addiction to alcohol, Proverbs 21:17 cautions against overeating, a particularly modern illness. High fat content foods other than olive oil would have been relatively rare in the average biblical person's diet. Only the wealthy could have afforded such a diet, and even they ate little meat when compared to modern consumption. Except on festive occasions (when they might kill the "fatted calf"), meat, if used at all, would be mainly a flavoring. To use a lot of oil would be comparable to a modern person indulging in rich and expensive foods, or eating constantly at expensive restaurants. Those with credit cards can soon discover how quickly one can run up a high balance just from eating out. The word "pleasure" in Proverbs 21:17 translates the same Hebrew word rendered "joy" in verse 15. Kidner says "the two sayings contrast two ways of life. The just man seeks to act fairly, and finds joy as he does so (15); the pleasure-lover strikes out towards joy itself, and finds poverty. Between the two verses comes the grim warning (16) that more than pleasure is at stake. Verses 20, 21, teach a similar lesson, materially and spiritually" (Kidner, p. 144). One cannot seek joy in wine.

[31] Whybray, p. 181.

[32] *Ibid.*, p. 138.

[33] Kidner, p. 153.

[34] Judith Sudilovsky, "Down the Hatch!" *Biblical Archaeology Review,* September/October, 1999, p. 18.

[35] Murphy states that according to the way the Masoretic scribes counted verses this is the central one of the book (*Proverbs,* p. 122).

[36] Proverbs 2 is a 22-line poem (the same number of lines as letters in the Hebrew alphabet) and forms one continuous conditional-type sentence (Murphy, *Proverbs,* p. 14).

[37] The fact that Proverbs has other interests than does a collection of books focusing on the deliverance of Israel and its preparation for the Promised Land, as well as the fact that the book of Proverbs consciously draws on the international wisdom tradition of the ancient Near East, can account for the different emphasis and perspective.

Chapter Five

CHOOSING THE TRUE PATH

As we saw in chapter 1, the people of the biblical era, including the Israelites, believed that the world had been made to function a certain way and that those who followed the natural or divinely ordained order would be successful in life. Those who ignored or rejected the cosmic principles would always find themselves in trouble. The wisdom tradition sought both to teach what the principles of life were and to encourage all to follow them.

In Proverbs 3:1, 2 the sage declares: "My child, do not forget my teaching,[1] but let your heart keep my commandments;[2] for length of days and years of life and abundant welfare they will give you."[3] The concept of following wise teachings that would lead to long life and prosperity appears several times in the book of Proverbs (for example, Prov. 4:10 and 5:1). A good reward for obedience is a frequent theme in the Old Testament even if it is not spelled out as clearly as it is here.

The sage asks his readers to obey "my teaching" (verse 1). "Teaching" translates the Hebrew word *torah*, often rendered as "law." Scholars still debate exactly what the term means, but most see in it elements of guidance, teaching, and instruction.[4] When *torah* appears without any qualifiers, as in Proverbs 28:9 and 29:18, it stands without question for God's law, but here the term refers to "the present maxims and to the home teachings, based instead upon the law, but not identical with it."[5] It is God's law as applied to the culture and situation of the sage and his time.

Those who seek wisdom should remain loyal and faithful to what they have learned through Israel's wise men. The sage says they should bind such teachings around their necks and write them on the tablet of their hearts, or as we would say today, inscribe them in their minds (Prov. 3:3). They should incorporate the teachings into their characters and lives. Doing so will bring them honor from both God and fellow human beings (verse 4).

To be truly wise, "trust in the Lord with all your heart, and do not rely on your own insight" (verse 5). Such trust in the Lord is a frequent refrain in the psalms and elsewhere in Scripture. If we will acknowledge God in everything we do, He will make the course of our lives straight and easy, unlike the rough roads that wound up and down across the rugged terrain of Palestine (verse 6). The passage's emphasis on trusting God instead of our own wisdom or intelligence is not, as it might seem at first, a rejection of the kind of wisdom the book of Proverbs itself advocates. Rather, "the truly wise person knows of limits. Wisdom is a gift of God (2:6), but whoever claims to be wise is more foolish than the fool (Prov. 26:12; cf. Jer. 9:22-23), and the next couplet (verses 7, 8) reinforces this idea. The Lord's role in the ways of humans is also indicated in 16:9 and 20:24 (cf. Hosea 14:10)."[6] Any spiritual insight or intelligence that we might have comes from God and must always remain under His guidance lest it deteriorate into folly.

Proverbs 4 portrays a father teaching his children wisdom. Boys and girls alike stayed under the close supervision of their mothers for the first few years of their life.[7] After that, the boys would enter the world of men, and their fathers would have a more active role in their instruction. Here the father urges his son to "get wisdom; get insight: do not forget, nor turn away from the words of my mouth" (verse 5). Obtaining wisdom, as we see in verses 5-9, is not an intellectual pursuit, but "a love engagement: one is to 'get,' 'love,' and 'embrace' wisdom beyond anything else. The intensity can be seen from the fourfold repetition of 'get.'"[8]

Since wisdom is a love relationship with God, so also obedience will reflect such a relationship. The passage apparently uses wedding imagery for "getting" wisdom. Whybray sees in verse 9 the custom of the bride placing a garland or crown on the bridegroom's head.[9] In essence, we marry wisdom, and our obedience to all commandments derived from it is as the relationship of a married couple to each other. Our obedience to God's torah is thus not an intellectual agreement, but a living and loving interaction with our God. Just as marriage is a constant choosing to be loyal to and trusting of each other, so we daily accept God's leading and guidance.

Proverbs 6:20 and 7:1-4 echo Proverbs 3:3, 4, using similar wording and imagery. Here we see that both parents participate in teaching wisdom (Prov. 6:20). All these references to the binding and writing of the commandments on the heart and tying them on the neck seem to be direct allusions to Deuteronomy 6:6-9 and 11:18-21. While Israelite wisdom may at times reflect the wider intellectual wisdom tradition of the ancient Near East, it has been carefully tied into the religion of Scripture. Biblical wisdom is not for the intellect's sake, but for God's sake. Wisdom's commandments will guide us in every aspect of life (Prov. 3:23, 24; 6:22).

What Is a Fool?

We have already encountered numerous references to the fool in the various sayings of the book of Proverbs. In this chapter we will examine a number of contrasts between those who observe the commandments and teachings of wisdom and those who do not. But first we must understand how the sage defines a fool. As we shall discover, Scripture classifies fools into several types, using specific terms for them and categorizing them by their behavior.

In common usage today the term *fool* often has the connotation of some kind of mental disability. But Scripture regards someone as a fool not on the basis of intelligence but on what the person does with it—how he or she behaves.

The Simple—Translators often render the Hebrew word *peti* as "simple." While such individuals may have adequate intelligence, they allow others to lead or trick them. They are gullible and perhaps even silly in their behavior and outlook. Naive, the *peti* will accept everything that others tell them. "The simple believe everything" (Prov. 14:15). "The clever see danger and hide; but the simple go on, and suffer for it" (Prov. 22:3). By "clever" the sage does not mean those with special skills or abilities, but rather those who live by the principles of wisdom. However, willfulness and irresponsibility get the "simple" into all kinds of trouble. "Waywardness kills the simple" (Prov. 1:32).

The book of Proverbs suggests that dramatic illustrations or examples may sometimes help these fools see the error of their ways. Perhaps if the *peti* observe what happens to others, they will stop and think about where they are heading. "Strike a scoffer,[10] and the simple will learn prudence" (Prov. 19:25). But if the *peti* refuse to open their eyes, they face a worse fate—they can slide into folly. Folly is premeditated rebellion against God and His principles of life. They and the *hasarleb*, or "senseless," consider their life of folly great "joy" or "fun" (Prov. 15:21). The "senseless" "follow worthless pursuits" (Prov. 12:11).

Proverbs 7 describes the "simple" "at his most typical: aimless, unexperienced, drifting into temptation—indeed almost courting it. A person in such a state (and the reader is not encouraged to think himself beyond such folly) will not go far before he meets a temptress, or (as in 1:10ff.) tempters, who know what they want and what he half wants. In short, the simple (and his elder brother, the fool) is no half-wit; he is a person whose instability could be rectified, but who prefers not to accept discipline in the school of wisdom (1:22-32)." [11]

The Fool—English-language Bibles generally translate three

Hebrew words as "fool." The most common, *kesil,* appears about 50 times in the book of Proverbs. The word seems to mean someone who is deliberately obtuse. While the *kesilim* may be bright enough, they refuse to discipline themselves so that they can profitably use their intelligence. They do not want to put forth the effort it takes to find God's wisdom. "The discerning person looks to wisdom, but the eyes of a fool to the ends of the earth" (Prov. 17:24).

"The fool is distracted and unfocused, looking everywhere, without ever fixing on the one thing that is necessary."[12] Their minds are everywhere except on what they should be doing— searching for wisdom. If they do show an interest in wisdom, they assume that it will be easy to obtain. Perhaps they think that they can purchase it like so much else in life. "Why should fools have a price in hand to buy wisdom, when they have no mind to learn?" (Prov. 17:16). "The point of this ironic proverb is to emphasize the hopeless situation of the fool. Even should he possess the means to become wise, he will not employ them."[13] Whybray observes that some people are born fools and not even education will give them wisdom.[14] It is not that education cannot help them, but that they refuse to let it transform them from their foolish state.

The *kesilim* babbles foolishly (Prov. 15:2), little realizing that they only expose their folly (Prov. 13:16). The sage says that the *kesilim* feed on folly, then, like those who have overgorged themselves, spew it back out of their mouths (Prov. 5:14). Even when the *kesilim* try to offer some proverbial wisdom, they mangle it—it comes out as useless as a crippled leg (Prov. 26:7), or even as dangerous as a viciously thorned bush waved around by a drunk (verse 9). And conceit totally blinds them (Prov. 17:10)

As appalling as the behavior of a fool may be, the *kesilim* actually like their folly. They have no desire to escape it, but constantly return to it like a dog does to its vomit (Prov. 26:11).[15] Their folly leads them into all kinds of fantasies and delusions

(Prov. 14:8). They can convince themselves of anything, no matter how preposterous. Because fools deceive themselves,[16] in the process they reject the only way to wisdom—the fear of the Lord (Prov. 1:29). Complacency destroys them (verse 32).

Fools of this type are not only dangerous to themselves, but also they threaten society as a whole. At the very least they waste people's time. The sage urges his readers not to hang around them. If life is a pursuit of wisdom and divine knowledge, fools are the very worst source for finding it (Prov. 14:7). In fact, they can even be dangerous. "Whoever walks with the wise becomes wise, but the companion of fools suffers harm" (Prov. 13:20). While the harm can be physical, financial, or social, it is always spiritually lethal.

Once an idea gets into the minds of the *kesilim,* nothing will stop them. "Better to meet a she-bear robbed of its cubs than to confront a fool immersed in folly" (Prov. 17:12). History is full of people who have plunged families, institutions, and even whole nations into ruin because of some obsession. Such fools destroy anyone who tries to warn them of the dangers of what they are doing. Folly becomes a game or sport to such fools (Prov. 10:23), no matter how bad what they do might be.

The word translated "wrong" by the NRSV means "sinful activity" in the Hebrew. "The point is the moral bankruptcy of the fool, who takes his wrongdoing as lightly as a joke."[17] Fools incite strife and social unrest (Prov. 18:6), and in the process they destroy themselves by their own words (verse 7).

It is bad enough just to encounter the *kesilim,* but to be related to one—especially as a parent—is especially tragic. The parent has to share in the dishonor of the fool. "What one member of the family was, every member of the family was, psychologically as well as in every other way."[18] Thus the presence of a fool in a family raises questions about the other members.

Ancient parents could not excuse their foolish offspring by blaming their behavior on bad genes or developmental stages. Society considered children to be simply an extension of the parents. Parents of fools experience grief (Prov. 10:1; 17:25), bitterness (Prov. 17:25), and ruin or tragedy (Prov. 19:13). Even a mother's love cannot reach them. The more parents love their foolish children, the more the fools despise them (Prov. 15:20).

The Eviylim—A related term for fool, the *eviyl*, appears 19 times in the book and is almost interchangeable with *kesil*.[19] The *eviylim* expose their foolishness the second they open their mouths (Prov. 10:14; 17:28; 24:7). Just as quarrelsome as the *kesilim* (Prov. 20:3), they will quickly explode in anger (Prov. 12:16). If you get caught in a legal dispute with them, expect only "ranting and ridicule without relief" (Prov. 29:9). And it will be displayed in public, since legal hearings took place at the city gate or in an open space in the market.

They are not interested in learning from others, only in tearing down others' ideas and beliefs. Nor do they want to discuss anything. The Hebrew of the latter part of Proverbs 29:9 literally means "and there is no quiet" or "quietness," thus allowing no opportunity for serious discussion.[20] The proverb may mean that the issue "will never be satisfactorily settled or that the fool will pour out a never-ending stream of *abuse* and *derision* in court."[21]

The *eviylim* reject all advice (Prov. 1:7; 10:8), even if it comes from a parent (Prov. 15:5), in a culture in which parents normally had great influence and respect. Such fools think they alone are right (Prov. 12:15). Society must deal with this folly as early as possible before it becomes permanent in the child (Prov. 22:15). The sage usually does not see much chance for changing a fool (Prov. 27:22) no matter how drastic the measures taken, "but if the young are trained early on, there is hope for them, as verse 6 also suggests. The training is inescapable if there is to be any change."[22] Such education must be firm, consistent, and unyielding. Sometimes highly structured environments such as military boot camps will reach such fools when nothing else will. At the same time fools must be taught self-control, or they will revert to their folly when once again they are on their own. But whatever the discipline, it must be serious yet loving.

The Nabalim—Appearing only three times in the book of Proverbs, the term *nabal* brings out the boorishness of the fool. They are crude and insensitive in their behavior. Whybray sees the point of the second line of Proverbs 30:22 as indicating that the *nabalim*, "being very unpleasant persons, ought to starve." [23]

Nabal appears elsewhere as the name of the wealthy man who rebuffed David's request for help in return for protection (1 Sam. 25:25) and in Psalm 14:1: "Fools say in their hearts, 'There is no God.' They are corrupt, they do abominable deeds." Derek Kidner calls the *nabal* an "overbearing, crudely godless man" [24] who has spurned the fundamental basis of true wisdom, the fear of the Lord. [25]

The Les—The final term that we will look at is the scoffer, *les*. Proverbs employs it 17 times, usually either in contrast with the wise or with one of the other terms for fool. The biblical writer especially uses it to indicate that attitude, not intelligence, defines a fool. [26] As with their fellow fools, scoffers dislike correction or discipline. When you rebuke them, they will abuse (Prov. 9:7) or hate you (verse 8) in return. Scoffers refuse to listen to correction (Prov. 13:1), because they simply don't like to be confronted when they do something wrong or foolish. They will, if at all possible, avoid the wise (Prov. 15:12). Their mindset makes it impossible for them to learn wisdom (Prov. 14:6). The scoffer is proud and haughty (Prov. 21:24) and creates continual strife, quarreling, and abuse (Prov. 22:10; 29:8).

Charming and persuasive at times, they will—unless you stop them—sway the gullible (Prov. 19:25; 21:11). Fortunately, many people of common sense will detect their true nature, finding them "an abomination" (Prov. 24:9). Eventually scoffers will receive their just punishment (Prov. 19:29). God bestows on them what they have done to others: "Toward the scorner [God] is scornful" (Prov. 3:34). "The punishment of the 'scoffers' is expressed in an unusual manner; the Lord pays them in kind. The sense [in Proverbs 3:34] is that he 'outscoffs' the scoffer (cf. Ps. 18:27)." [27]

Fundamental Characteristics of the Fool

The book of Proverbs points out a number of traits common to all fools. For example, besides being arrogant and self-centered, they are emotional time bombs ready to explode at the slightest provocation (Prov. 14:17, 29; 29:11). Fools enjoy quarrels and fights (Prov. 20:3). Instead of seeking advice from others, they rely on their own knowledge and reasoning (Prov. 12:15; 28:26), considering themselves "wise in their own eyes" (Prov. 26:5). Their greatest problem is lack of self-control, whether it be of their behavior and feelings (Prov. 12:23) or of what they blurt out (Prov. 10:14; 17:28; 18:13).

Scripture views fools as those in total rebellion against God and the way He created us to live. In many ways fools reflect the character and rebellion of Satan himself. Being a fool is not a charge to hurl lightly against another. Perhaps this helps us understand why Jesus warns us against calling someone a fool lest we wind up in hellfire (Matt. 5:22). It is difficult for one human being to determine the motivations of others, and calling someone a fool is comparing the individual to Satan. By doing that we may be consigning ourselves to the hellfire reserved for the devil himself (Matt. 25:41), just as those in the Old Testament who falsely accused someone had to suffer the punishment of the alleged crime. With the aid of the Holy Spirit we can recognize the fool in ourselves, but we had best leave determining the state of others to God.

Contrasting the Wise and the Fool

A basic aspect of many proverbial sayings is that of contrasting one thing with another. The book of Proverbs repeatedly emphasizes the fundamental difference in direction between the life of the wise person and that of the fool. Proverbs 13 and 15, for example, offer a series of such contrasts. Many of them focus on what happens to those who keep God's teachings as opposed to those who reject God's commandments.

Fools bring destruction upon themselves when they ignore

God's revelation, whereas the wise receive reward (Prov. 13:13). The wise teach others how to escape the snares of death, both literally and spiritually (verse 14), but by implication the fools leap into those same snares. Anyone who exhibits that rarest of all commodities—good sense—will naturally receive honor from others, but those who are faithless face only ruin (verse 15). The clever do all things thoughtfully, while the foolish impetuously blurt out folly (verse 16). Poverty and disgrace await those who ignore divine teaching, but those who listen to reproof will receive that most desired reward in Mediterranean society—honor (verse 18).

The person without sense blithely wanders in folly, but the wise walk straight ahead under divine direction (Prov. 15:21). Plans carefully made with the guidance of others will succeed, but the harebrained schemes of those who refuse to listen to counsel will only fail (verse 22). Fools come to ruin because they depend upon themselves, a most unreliable source of aid. They are out of sync with the way God designed the universe to function.

The only way they can succeed is to get back in phase with divine reality, and that involves listening to and obeying God's revealed wisdom. They must let the Lord show them the true path to walk in. To do that, they must have the fear of the Lord, which brings countless benefits. It prolongs life in contrast to the short existence of the wicked (Prov. 10:27).[28] The righteous will have their hope fulfilled in gladness,[29] while the dreams of the wicked will come to nothing (verse 28). The way of the Lord will protect the righteous (using the image of a fortress) but will destroy those who reject it (verse 29).[30]

Storms may rage through life, yet "when the tempest passes, the wicked are no more, but the righteous are established forever" (verse 25). "The righteous will never be removed, but the wicked will not remain in the land" (verse 30).[31]

All the disasters that strike fools originate with their own doing. They have chosen a direction in life that can lead only to ultimate ruin, and they have no one to blame but themselves.

"The iniquities of the wicked ensnare them, and they are caught in the toils of their sin. They die for lack of discipline, and because of their great folly they are lost" (Prov. 5:22, 23). The harvest that comes after sowing injustice is calamity (Prov. 22:8). Rebellion, especially against God, can lead only to sure punishment (Prov. 17:11). The wicked may for a time get away with the strife and discord they create, but it will all backfire on them in the end (Prov. 6:12-15).

The Fate of the Fool

Wisdom literature in general attempted to teach a person how to live prosperously, how to make the best of one's station in life.[32] Biblical wisdom, however, sought a successful life on a more spiritual and cosmic plane. Such success was not determined by what others thought, as in non-Israelite wisdom tradition, but by God Himself, since "human ways are under the eyes of the Lord, and he examines all their paths" (Prov. 5:21). The Lord of the universe, like Anubis of Egyptian mythology, weighs the heart and repays all according to their deeds (Prov. 24:12). If He will reward the righteous, just as surely will He punish the sinner (Prov. 11:31). They who have rebelled so long will be "broken beyond healing" (Prov. 29:1) as He demolishes the house of the proud (Prov. 15:25; 21:12).

The ultimate fate that befalls each of us is our own choice to make. While many of the events of this life may be beyond our control, our spiritual direction is always ours to decide. But to make that decision correctly, we must have wisdom—wisdom that comes solely through God's revelation and divine teaching.

"Listen to advice and accept instruction," the biblical sage urges, "that you may gain wisdom for the future" (Prov. 19:20; cf. 12:15; 23:12). Here the sage may have in mind only this life, but the rest of Scripture reveals that this life is not all there is, that the injustice overlooked in the present existence will be dealt with in the next. We may not always see the consequences of our choices in the here and now, but they will receive their reward or punishment in the future life. If we walk in the way of wisdom now, we will stride hereafter with God for eternity. But if we choose the direction of folly, we will truly discover that it is only a dead end.

---

[1] The high value placed here on the teacher's words echoes that of such Egyptian documents as the *Instruction of Amenemope,* though it does appear in essence elsewhere in the Old Testament (R.N. Whybray, *The Book of Proverbs,* p. 24).

[2] Compare *Instruction of Amenemope* 3:11 and Jeremiah 31:33 (*ibid.,* p. 25).

[3] Compare *Instruction of Amenemope* 4:1, 2 *(ibid.).*

[4] *Dictionary of Biblical Imagery,* p. 489.

[5] Derek Kidner, *Proverbs,* p. 63.

[6] Roland E. Murphy, *Proverbs,* p. 21.

[7] Bruce J. Malina and Richard L. Rohrbaugh, *Social-Science Commentary on the Gospel of John,* pp. 272, 273.

[8] Murphy, *Proverbs,* p. 27.

[9] Whybray, p. 30.

[10] Another category of fool.

[11] Kidner, p. 39.

[12] Murphy, *Proverbs,* p. 131.

[13] Ibid., p. 130.

[14] Whybray, p. 101.

[15] Gross though the image may be to modern-day dog lovers, the ancients regarded the creature as a half-wild scavenger and tolerated it only because it disposed of some of the garbage dumped around a village.

[16] Murphy, *Proverbs,* p. 104.

[17] *Ibid.,* p. 75.

[18] Malina and Rohrbaugh, *Social-Science Commentary on the Synoptic Gospels,* p. 113.

[19] Kidner, p. 41.

[20] R.B.Y. Scott, *Proverbs/Ecclesiastes,* p. 170.

[21] Whybray, p. 168.

[22] Murphy, *Proverbs,* p. 166.

[23] Whybray, p. 178.

[24] Kidner, p. 123.

[25] *Ibid.,* p. 41.

[26] *Ibid.*

[27] Murphy, *Proverbs,* p. 23.

[28] The Old Testament is strongly this-life centered and has relatively little to say about the future life. The book of Proverbs is no exception, and it has nothing clear-cut to say about what happens after death. The goal it focuses on is long and prosperous years in this existence.

[29] The hope of the righteous will never be cut off (Murphy, *Proverbs*, p. 76). Cf. Prov. 23:18; 24:14.

[30] Murphy sees "way" here as possibly referring to both "God's general way of acting, protecting the just," and the "way of wisdom" of Proverbs 4:11 (*ibid.*, p. 76).

[31] "Remain in the land" echoes phraseology from the Pentateuch, another strand of Israelite religion woven into the wisdom tradition.

[32] Unlike modern Western society, few in the ancient world imagined that they could climb to a higher position in life. Commenting on Egyptian civilization, for example, Joyce Tyldesley writes: "At all times there was remarkably little movement between the classes, and it was very difficult for anyone, male or female, to advance from one social group to another" (Joyce Tyldesley, *Daughters of Isis: Women of Ancient Egypt*, p. 14).

Chapter Six

THE PATH TO TRUE WEALTH

If in recent years you turned on the television late at night or during the early-morning hours in North America, it seemed as if almost every channel has had an infomercial promoting some scheme to get rich quick. The pitches varied from investing in foreclosed real estate to buying precious metals to making a killing on the stock market. Publishers have deluged the bookstores with volumes claiming to reveal the secret of how to retire early and live the good life. Emerging nations set up pyramid schemes that ultimately collapsed and cost the life savings of hundreds of thousands of citizens. But the desire to get rich is not new. It has always tempted human beings—even in the simpler world of the Bible.

Proverbs 28:20 warns that "one who is in a hurry to be rich will not go unpunished." Modern men and women would find the idea of being punished for getting rich quickly rather startling and uncomfortable. Verse 22 adds that "the miser is in a hurry to get rich and does not know that loss is sure to come." Today we admire people who become rich, especially if they can do it quickly enough to retire young enough to enjoy it. Everyone would like to acquire wealth. As the character Tevye in *Fiddler on the Roof* asks, Would it disturb some cosmic plan if we could be rich?

The ancient biblical world had two minds on the subject of wealth. On the one hand, it saw riches as a sign of God's blessing. On the other hand, it distrusted those who were wealthy because the suspicion was that they got their wealth dishonestly. It is important for us to observe how the economic situation of Bible times differed from that of the financial world today. This fundamental difference will help us understand why many—especially in the New Testament—distrusted those driven by the desire to become rich.

Modern men and women can become entrepreneurs, starting a business that meets some real or imagined customer need. We can invest in stocks and bonds, letting the magic of compound interest grow us a respectable nest egg. Or we can, like Bill Gates and other computer pioneers, develop a new technology that revolutionizes the world. How would the world today survive without computer technology? We can almost create fortunes out of thin air.

Wealth in the Ancient World

But the economy of the ancient world was quite different. The basis of almost all wealth back then was ownership of land. (Fishing was one of the few exceptions, though one might argue that the seas, rivers, and lakes were just land covered with water.) People grew crops and herded flocks on it, cut lumber or stone from it, and mined minerals within its bowels. Land was in a limited supply, especially land suitable for farming. Thus people conceived of trade and commerce as a "limited good" economy.

According to Bruce J. Malina and Richard L. Rohrbaugh, the people of Palestine thought that "all goods existed in finite, limited supply and were already distributed. This included not only material goods, but honor, friendship, love, power, security, and status as well—literally everything in life. Because the pie could not grow larger, a larger piece for anyone automatically meant a smaller piece for someone else."[1]

Today we would expand the production line for more consumer goods or create more awards to honor more people. But the ancients could not imagine expanding the economy. (If we were really honest, even today we would have to admit that our resources are still finite. They are just bigger than those of the ancient world and exploited in different ways.)

Thus the only way to get rich was to take from someone else. If the basis of wealth was land, to become wealthier meant that others had to lose their land—and consequently their source of livelihood. The average family supported itself on what they could grow and manufacture on their bit of land. There were no factory jobs to provide employment away from the land. The few wealthy families might buy luxury goods, but not enough to maintain a middle class of any size. Biblical society consisted of the majority of poor and a few privileged families.[2]

One person's gain always led to someone else's loss. Crop failure often drove a family to borrow food and seed at exorbitant rates. Ancient Near Eastern documents record interest rates of 20 to 50 percent. Eventually families found themselves forced to sell their land—and sometimes even themselves into slavery. Unscrupulous large-scale landowners took advantage of the situation. As we see happening again in the world today, the rich get richer and the poor ever poorer. The erosion of high-paying jobs in the industrialized West is erasing the middle class that developed during the past century.

The Old Testament records many laws and stories concerning the loss of land and the peasant's slide into desperate poverty.[3] By New Testament times biblical society felt that it was almost impossible for a rich person to be saved. After all, wealthy individuals were either dishonest or their ancestors had been. How else could they have gotten rich? "Profit making and the acquisition of wealth were automatically assumed to be the result of extortion or fraud, and the notion of an honest rich man was a first-century oxymoron."[4]

In the book of Proverbs the problem of the rich and poor

during biblical times had not yet deteriorated to the condition we find in the New Testament. However, many of the forces were already at work, and we must keep them in mind as we study what the biblical writer has to say about riches and poverty, especially as we try to apply the counsel to our modern situation.

The scribe in proverbs often reveals a hostility toward those who act in haste.[5] Haste could be a dangerous trait in small enclosed societies (including modern churches and religious groups). And that included getting rich quickly. "Whatever is associated with haste always seems suspect to the sage. This view is particularly applicable to riches; haste might imply a lack of appreciation for wealth, or more likely it suggests some kind of disreputable action, perhaps at the expense of others; cf. Proverbs 20:21; 28:20b; 22a."[6] One might accumulate wealth slowly through hard work and shrewd economy, but the only way to get it quickly was through theft or some other questionable activity.

In the end such craving for riches will become destructive to the person who harbored it. "No matter the cautions he takes, he will lose in the end because that is the way retribution works."[7] Justice will punish those who stole from or defrauded others. Better to acquire wealth slowly and carefully. While "wealth hastily gotten will dwindle, . . . those who gather little by little will increase it" (Prov. 13:11; cf. Prov. 21:5). As we noted already, wealth accumulated slowly most likely came through honest methods as well as by plain hard work.[8] Today we debate "conservative" versus "aggressive" approaches to investment strategy, but some of the same cautions might still apply.

In the biblical world being rich or poor involved more than the size of one's bank account or investment portfolio. "To be labeled 'rich' was . . . a social and moral statement as much as an economic one. It meant having the power or capacity to take from someone weaker what was rightfully his. Being rich was synonymous with being greedy. By the same token, being 'poor' was to be unable to defend what was yours. It meant falling below the status at which one was born. It was to be defenseless, without recourse."[9]

Although Malina and Rohrbaugh are speaking of the New Testament situation, the conditions that they refer to were, as we already said, the outcome of forces already at work in the Old Testament. The laws of the Pentateuch tried to slow them, the prophets protested them, and Nehemiah had to deal with the vast gulf between rich and poor after the Exile. The people of the Old Testament might have seen wealth as the clear sign of God's blessing, but a counteropinion was developing that would turn into the New Testament prejudice against the rich.[10]

This moral tone toward the categories rich and poor shines through in such passages as Proverbs 28:6: "Better to be poor and walk in integrity than to be crooked in one's ways even though rich." The biblical sage would counsel "do not wear yourself out to get rich; be wise enough to desist" (Prov. 23:4) for many reasons. "There are many sayings about riches in the book, but this one is unique in that it warns directly *against* them, and on the basis of wisdom! They can become an all-consuming purpose in life; and also frustrating because they can disappear so easily."[11]

Do we examine the ethical basis of our financial dealings today? Do we check to see if our investments support companies that hurt the poor, especially in the developing world?

Does a company we buy from prosper through exploiting its employees? Should a Christian purchase products made under sweatshop conditions or grown on land defrauded from its original owners? And what about us—has getting rich become an all-consuming passion?

Avoidable Poverty

While most people in the ancient Near East slid into poverty because of forces outside their control, some caused their own fate through the lifestyle they chose to live. Laziness could plunge a person into poverty. The book has much to say about the slothful (Prov. 12:24, 27; 15:19; 18:9; 19:15, 24; 21:25; 22:13; 24:30-34) and the sluggard (Prov. 6:6, 9; 10:26; 13:3; 20:4; 25:16).[12]

Lazy people are not only a hazard to themselves but are also irritants to others: "Like vinegar to the teeth and smoke to the eyes, so are the lazy to their employers" (Prov. 10:26). Talking instead of working could lead to poverty (Prov. 14:23). Dreaming of impractical goals and dabbling in unrealistic schemes can destroy us financially: "Anyone who tills the land will have plenty of bread, but one who follows worthless pursuits will have plenty of poverty" (Prov. 28:19). An ancient Egyptian scribe echoed the same theme when he said: "Plow your fields and you'll find what you need, you'll receive bread from your threshing-floor."[13] In other words, keep on doing what you're best at and don't put your faith in half-baked get-rich schemes or anything else that attempts to substitute for honest hard work.

"Anyone who tends a fig tree will eat its fruit" (Prov. 27:18). Do your work and it will reward you, but if you don't, you must expect the consequences—poverty. "A little sleep, a little slumber, a little folding of the hands to rest, and poverty will come upon you like a robber, and want, like an armed warrior" (Prov. 6:10, 11).

One of the most dangerous routes to poverty is getting involved in someone else's financial affairs or problems. Proverbs 6:1-5 warns against becoming surety for another's debt. Many even today, out of a desire to be helpful, cosign a loan for a good friend, only to have the other person default. They then find themselves saddled with unexpected debt. The biblical sage urges any person who has fallen into such a predicament to get out of it as quickly as possible, even if they have to plead with the individual for a release (verse 3). Don't stop until you have extricated yourself (verse 4).

Also, if possible avoid debt of any kind, because "the borrower is the slave of the lender" (Prov. 22:7). Unfortunately, that was sometimes impossible. The ancient peasant might have to borrow just to survive. He would need grain to feed his family after a disastrous crop failure and seed to plant with the next growing season. It is a bad situation when you find yourself forced to borrow food money. That is why the Old Testament forbade the charging of interest to fellow Israelites (Ex. 22:25; Deut. 23:19; Eze. 18:18). They were family, and family shared.

In North America borrowing has become a way of life. Credit card companies particularly target the young in school. Before young people realize it they have rung up massive debt loads. Some, unable to face what they have done, have committed suicide. Others have begun their new adult lives by declaring bankruptcy. Millions have sold their future into slavery for briefly enjoying the good life now.

The Rich and the Poor

That society has both the rich and the poor might be a fact of life, but that does not mean that it is right. "The wealth of the rich is their fortress; the poverty of the poor is their ruin" (Prov. 10:15; cf. Prov. 18:11). The rich can become hopelessly trapped in their castle of riches, though finances involve more than just the effects of selfishness on the rich man or woman. There is the problem of the inequality of wealth's distribution. But God can overrule the injustice of life. A person may accumulate great wealth through charging exorbitant interest, for example, but God in His providence may direct it to someone more kind to the poor (Prov. 28:8). "The unspoken motivation [in Proverbs 28:8] is that the Lord will act, and prevent the unjust dealer from enjoying his ill-gotten profits. Instead they will be turned to the advantage of a generous person; cf. Proverbs 14:31; 19:17." [14] As Proverbs 13:22 says, "the sinner's wealth is laid up for the righteous." It may take a long time and may not be recognized in this life, but when seen from the perspective of eternity, God restores the wealth extorted from the poor. But He would rather have the rich share by their own free choice.

"Those who oppress the poor insult their Maker," the sage

states, "but those who are kind to the needy honor him" (Prov. 14:31). Roland Murphy reminds us: "The religious and ethical basis for one's relationship to the poor is undeniable, and it is developed at length in Deuteronomy 15:1-11. The 'his' in 'his maker' can refer to both the oppressor as well as to the oppressed; after all, God made them both (22:2)." [15]

"The duty of kindness to the *poor* is recognized in the ethical codes of many peoples including those of the ancient Near East; but the motive given here, which is also found in [Prov.] 17:5 and Job 31:15, seems to be an original contribution of Israelite wisdom literature. . . . It is characteristic of Jewish wisdom literature that it took the doctrine of creation very seriously as a theological concept. Jesus in his teaching (Matt. 25:31-46) takes the idea further still: 'Anything you did for one of my brothers here, however humble, you did for me' (verse 40)." [16]

Just as Christ did in the New Testament, so God had already done in the Old Testament: He identified Himself with the poor. "Whoever is kind to the poor lends to the Lord" (Prov. 19:17). "The implication is that God will repay the loan—with interest!" [17] But as Derek Kidner cautions, "it promises faithful recompense, not necessarily one's money back!" [18] The book of Proverbs implies that the reward may come in this life, while the New Testament teaches that we will primarily receive it in heaven. But God does promise to reward.

Sharing With the Poor

God wants us to share with others what He has blessed us with. But how we do it is our choice. We can give liberally or grudgingly. "Some give freely, yet grow all the richer; others withhold what is due, and only suffer want. A generous person will be enriched, and one who gives water will get water" (Prov. 11:24, 25). In a land of few flowing streams and limited springs and wells, a gift of water meant much more than it does to us who just have to turn on a faucet. Whatever we give, God does a strange thing from the human perspective. The more water we give others, the more water we find in the well.

"The people curse those who hold back grain, but a blessing is on the head of those who sell it" (verse 26). It's a fundamental concept of business to hold on to a commodity in short supply until the price peaks to make as much profit as possible. "Those who refuse to sell [the grain], because of a famine or any other reason, are profiting from a future rise in value—and the hardship they cause merits a curse. In contrast, the generous who will forego profit for the sake of the common good will receive a 'blessing' that will be more tangible than popularity or fond memory (10:7), presumably from God." [19]

It was the moral duty of those who had reserves of grain to put it on the market.[20] The righteous never take advantage of those in need. They care for them as does God—they are His hands on earth. God blesses those who share their food with the poor (Prov. 22:9). Those who give to the poor will not lack, but those who ignore need will receive curses from those around them—and by implication, from God Himself (Prov. 28:27). God expects all His people to protect the poor and needy (Prov. 31:9). Sharing with others teaches us how to love like God and breaks down our barriers of selfishness.

Both the rich and the poor have the same Creator and God (Prov. 22:2). Although biblical society toyed with the idea that wealth is a sign of God's approval and blessing for some time, such passages as these undermine the deterministic theory of reward and punishment. In the New Testament Christ shows God's love for the poor and disadvantaged. Jesus brought good news to the poor (Luke 4:18) and pronounced them blessed, or honored (Luke 6:20), instead of cursed. The Gospel of Luke especially shows His concern for the poor. The Christian church would continue that care. James could ask: "Has not God chosen the poor in the world to be rich in faith and to be heirs of the kingdom that he has promised to those who love him?" (James 2:5). He has more in mind here than spiritual poverty.

Wealth and God

The Bible presents only one way that wealth will not destroy its recipient. The wealthy must always acknowledge that riches come ultimately from God, and that they must use it in ways that honor Him. "Honor the Lord with your substance and with the first fruits of all your produce; then your barns will be filled with plenty, and your vats will be bursting with wine" (Prov. 3:9, 10).[21] "To 'know' God in our financial 'ways' is to see that they *honour* Him; the honour will be compounded largely of homage (in giving Him the first and not a later share, 9; cf. 1 Cor. 16:2; Mark 12:44), of gratitude (see Deut. 26:9-11) and of trust (cf. verse 5), for such giving in the face of material pressures is a simple test of faith. But a basic ingredient is fair business dealings; and this is saved up for fuller treatment in the final paragraph (27-35)."[22]

The Egyptian wisdom book *The Instruction of Ani* also advised honoring one's god.[23] But the Bible depicts homage as more than just sacrifices. We honor God with everything we are and do—our whole lives, including our wealth, talents, and deeds.

Wealth can bring heartache as well as happiness. For most people it is the former. Only those who honor and worship God will find riches a true blessing. The New Revised Standard Version translates Proverbs 10:22: "The blessing of the Lord makes rich, and he adds no sorrow with it." Roland Murphy renders it: "The blessing of the Lord—that brings riches, and no toil can add to it."[24] Whichever translation we follow, one thing is clear: Only God can give us true wealth. And only He enables us to use it properly—to His honor and glory.

---

[1] Bruce J. Malina and Richard L. Rohrbaugh, *Social-Science Commentary on the Synoptic Gospels,* p. 48.

[2] For a discussion of the "limited good" economy and how it shaped society, see Malina and Rohrbaugh, *Synoptic Gospels,* pp. 48, 49, 251, 252, 324, 325.

[3] I have discussed some of these issues in *Beyond Life: What God Says About Life, Death, and Immortality* (Hagerstown, Md.: Review and Herald Pub. Assn., 1998), pp. 31-39.

[4] Malina and Rohrbaugh, *Synoptic Gospels,* p. 25.

[5] Roland E. Murphy, *Proverbs*, p. 217.

[6] *Ibid.*, p. 97.

[7] *Ibid.*, p. 217.

[8] "Compare this saying, however, with 28:20, where it seems to be implied that it is impossible to make a quick fortune honestly" (R. N. Whybray, *The Book of Proverbs*, p. 78).

[9] Malina and Rohrbaugh, *Synoptic Gospels*, p. 48.

[10] Passages such as Matthew 19:24 bother the modern Western mind. We try to explain them away. But the negative attitude toward the wealthy pervades the New Testament. And the average person had plenty of reason to distrust the rich and question their morals and ethics.

[11] Murphy, *Proverbs*, p. 175.

[12] Modern English translations usually render the KJV "slothful" and "sluggard" with such words as "lazy" and "lazybones."

[13] Miriam Lichtheim, *Ancient Egyptian Literature*, Vol. II, p. 152.

[14] Murphy, *Proverbs*, p. 215.

[15] *Ibid.*, p. 107.

[16] Whybray, p. 85.

[17] Murphy, *Proverbs*, p. 145.

[18] Derek Kidner, *Proverbs*, p. 134.

[19] Murphy, *Proverbs*, p. 84.

[20] Whybray, p. 69.

[21] The wine in the vats is unfermented grape juice. See Murphy, *Proverbs*, p. 21.

[22] Kidner, p. 64.

[23] See Lichtheim, Vol. II, p. 136.

[24] Murphy, *Proverbs*, p. 70.

THE PATH OF INTEGRITY

Ancient Near Eastern religion often lacked a strong ethical sense. It focused on meeting the gods' needs and, especially in Egypt, ensuring that they kept the universe from collapsing back into primeval chaos. The gods themselves were not role models for moral behavior. They lied, cheated, committed rape and adultery, and murdered in their struggles for dominance. Nor did they particularly care what their worshipers did as long as human beings did not directly offend the gods themselves.

In Egypt, for example, the state religion had no creed or moral or pastoral elements. It served primarily as a way of uniting a nation and had comparatively little interest in transforming the people spiritually. "Although it was generally accepted that men and women should choose to lead a good life rather than a bad one, this moral code evolved more for the convenience of society than the gratification of the gods. Virtue did not necessarily reap any heavenly reward, and only the king was required to act in a fitting and proper manner to ensure the preservation of *maat* throughout the land. The gods themselves showed remarkably little concern over the behaviour of the ordinary Egyptians, although when directly provoked they could retaliate with a vengeance."[1]

Israelite religion, however, was greatly concerned with how people—including the ordinary person—lived and behaved. Scripture constantly calls for human beings to lead moral and ethical lives. It expects them to seek and live out the principles of righteousness. The book of Proverbs is no exception. After urging his readers to seek wisdom (Prov. 2:1-4), the sage promises that they "will understand the fear of the Lord and find the knowledge of God" (verse 5). The Lord gives wisdom to the righteous (verse 6), and, in addition, He "is a shield to those who walk blamelessly, guarding the paths of justice and preserving the way of his faithful ones" (verses 7, 8).

The Lord of Israel is not a distant deity, but comes close to His people. He helps them live out the principles of His wisdom. "To 'understand' these virtues is to put them into practice."[2] Derek Kidner observes that the sequence of moral-oriented nouns leaves no doubt that the goal of wisdom is right conduct.[3] The God of the Bible is not only interested in how His people behave, He also enables them to live righteously.

Scripture demands integrity of all people. This God-given gift guides the righteous (Prov. 11:3), keeping the paths of their lives straight (verse 5),[4] and saving them from sin's destruction (verse 6). The wicked, on the other hand, find themselves trapped by their own schemes (verse 6). Their wickedness causes their fall (verse 5) and destruction (verse 3). They and their hope perish, and their dreams and goals come to nothing (verse 7).[5]

Those who seek wisdom will live moral and ethical lives patterned after the morality and ethics of their God. He desires integrity at all levels of society, beginning with leadership.

The Integrity of Leadership

Humanity has always struggled with the problem of morally and ethically corrupt leadership. The recent scandals in various world governments are nothing new. The blight strikes every organization, including religion. Even church leaders have recently found themselves convicted in criminal court cases. It has become so bad that many just shrug off the headlines and ignore the whole issue.

Even in his time the sage of the book of Proverbs had to plead for moral leadership by reminding that "when the righteous are in authority, the people rejoice; but when the wicked rule, the people groan" (Prov. 29:2). The inhabitants of a country have to hide when the wicked gain power, but righteous leadership leads to a prosperous nation (Prov. 28:12, 28). Transgression of every kind increases under a corrupt government (Prov. 29:16).

God wants government and all other kinds of leadership to be honest, moral, and righteous. They should reflect the principles of divine wisdom—wisdom that comes from the Ruler of the entire universe. The sage says that loyalty and faithfulness will protect the king (Prov. 20:28). Whybray points out that both terms belong to the vocabulary of treaties and covenants.[6] The king should rule according to the principles of the covenant that God established with David and his descendants. With wisdom as its foundation, any government will have a strong foundation. It will be able to withstand rebellion and revolution. In fact, such things are less likely to arise under a righteous leadership.

But "it is an abomination for kings to do evil, for the throne is established by righteousness" (Prov. 16:12). "The use of 'abomination,' which is most often used of the Lord, indicates how far from the king must be any hint of injustice. In fact, justice is what secures the throne; the idea is repeated in 20:8; 25:5; 29:14."[7]

Instead of tolerating evil, government should work to eradicate it. The king must winnow it from his kingdom as he would chaff and pebbles from grain (Prov. 20:8, 26). But to rule righteously, all leaders must surround themselves with wise and moral counselors. History is an endless recitation of what happens when corrupt advisers influence government. Such individuals must be removed (Prov. 25:5).

A just government is a stable one, but those that run

roughshod over their citizens, especially in the area of taxation, will slide into chaos and collapse (Prov. 29:4). We could cite endless examples of rulers who exploited the people to fund massive building projects or wars of conquest. Herod, for example, bled his people to construct not only the Temple in Jerusalem but also monuments throughout the Roman Empire. Some of them were even temples to pagan gods. The prophet Samuel had warned God's people of such exploitation when they demanded a king (1 Sam. 8:11-18).

Leadership must avoid favoring wealth or any other vested interest. A king that judges the poor with equity will ensure the security of his throne (Prov. 29:14). But he must do more than judge them fairly. He must especially look out for their interests. "A duty of the king is care for the poor, but no impartiality is to be permitted on this level. There is no official 'option for the poor,' but the juxtaposition of verses 13, 14 is significant. It is the responsibility of the king to insure justice for those who are least likely to be heard. The stability of the throne is made dependent upon this royal conduct."[8]

Social justice is a dominant theme of the Old Testament. The Pentateuch lists numerous laws to protect the poor and disadvantaged. The prophets protest the exploitation of the poor. And a concern for the poor appears here in the wisdom literature. Proverbs 31:1-9 has the mother of King Lemuel counseling her son on how to rule. Among other charges, she urges him to "speak out for those who cannot speak, for the rights of all the destitute. Speak out, judge righteously, defend the rights of the poor and needy" (Prov. 31:8, 9). She wants him to uphold the "socially weak," those "without a voice among those who administer justice. Here the king is to enter in favor of the 'dispossessed.' . . . The Hebrew phrase for this class has been interpreted to refer to orphans, or particularly unfortunate people in society. Despite the vagueness, it is clear that those who need help to establish their rights are meant."[9] The king was the supreme judge of the land, the court of last resort. All appeals came to him. We see his judicial function in such biblical incidents as those recorded in 2 Samuel 14:4-11 and 1 Kings 3:16-28. Since he was the court of last resort, he must be especially just and concerned about those on the margins of society.

The sage declares in Proverbs 16:10 that a king's decision shall be "inspired"[10] and that he should never sin in judgment. The king may have great authority, but he must always judge on a human level the same way God does on the divine. Human justice should reflect the heavenly courtroom, and the king must answer to the heavenly Judge. Too often human leadership forgets that it must answer to a higher authority. Power feeds the self-centeredness lurking in each of us.

Rulers set the example for integrity, but the whole society is to follow their example. All—both high and low—must live out the principles of wisdom. And justice is one of its most vital principles.

Justice—The Foundation of Society

Injustice has plagued every society. Life is complex, human knowledge is always incomplete, and human wisdom is finite. It is easy to make mistakes when judging situations. But the deliberate distortion of justice has been one of humanity's greatest failings. One part of society will seek justice for itself, while another more powerful segment will pervert it for its own interests. Those with wealth, position, and influence can sway the decision in their favor. The poor and the powerless find themselves taken advantage of. If society allows injustice to continue to grow, it will soon lead to collapse, as we see illustrated in the great rebellions and revolutions that have swept across many nations. To prevent this, the biblical sage calls for true justice.

"It is not right to be partial to the guilty," Proverbs warns, "or to subvert the innocent in judgment" (Prov. 18:5). "To show favor or partiality is literally 'to lift up the face' of the one who is favored. It reflects a situation in which a superior instructs an inferior, who has bowed down, to stand up, and thus he lifts up the face.[11] Here it describes the action of a judge who blatantly issues an unjust decision; cf. 17:23."[12]

Whybray sees Proverbs 18:5 as equivalent to such Old Testament laws as Deuteronomy 1:16, 17; 10:17, 18; 16:19; and Exodus 23:6-8 forbidding partiality in legal proceedings.[13] Although the judge must protect the rights of the poor and show a concern for their needs, this did not demand that the court must always rule in their favor. True justice meant showing them no undue partiality either (Ex. 23:2, 3; Lev. 19:15). Each case must be decided on its own merits.

Proverbs takes a strong stand against the abuse of justice in a world that dispensed one kind of justice for the wealthy and another, harsher form for the poor. The Mesopotamian law codes indicated that what might cost the rich only a fine, the poor might have to pay with their lives. "Partiality in judging is not good. Whoever says to the wicked, 'You are innocent,' will be cursed by peoples, abhorred by nations; but those who rebuke the wicked will have delight, and a good blessing will come upon them" (Prov. 24:23-25). The sage took it for granted that all civilized nations share certain ethical principles[14] and that they would be aghast at the perversion of justice.

True justice will bring joy to the righteous and dismay to the wicked (Prov. 21:15). It will reject all forms of bribery (Prov. 17:23). Such bribery does not have to be money, but can be favors or offers of prestige and preferment.

Deceit and Dishonesty

Closely allied with injustice is the problem of deceit and dishonesty. Crooked judges can be deceitful or lie during legal proceedings, but the twin traits have spread to all aspects of life. Public surveys in Western countries have revealed a startling willingness to lie or cheat, whether it be on school tests, paying taxes, or anything else. Many cultures see nothing wrong with lying. The only shame comes at getting caught doing it. Advertising, politics, and international relations often build on dishonesty and deceit.

The wicked dwell in a world of deceit and intrigue (Prov. 12:20) and offer treacherous advice (verse 5). They tell others what they want to hear or what will be to their advantage. They so distort reality that nothing seems what it is. But all that the wicked gain comes at a terrible price—what may seem sweet at first will have a horrible aftertaste as life reduces them to groveling (Prov. 20:17; cf. 9:17). R.B.Y. Scott suggests that the wicked man's mouth is full of gravel because retribution has forced him to lie on the ground in total defeat and submission.[15]

Even associating with those who practice evil has its consequences. It taints one's character and destroys self-respect. Proverbs 29:24, using the example of a thief, declares cryptically: "To be a partner of a thief is to hate one's own life;[16] one hears the victim's curse, but discloses nothing." "Consorting with a thief implies sharing in unlawful deeds and their fruits, and it is self-destructive. The 'curse' in verse 24b is to be understood in the light of the legislation of Leviticus 5:1-5. The law required that those who know of a crime must give witness; an oath is laid upon such to do so. If they keep silent, despite 'hearing' the oath invoked upon them, they are as guilty as the thief."[17] Those who hide guilty secrets, whether it be of someone else's wicked deeds or their own sinful behavior, have to live a lie that eats away at their moral character. Experience often shows that the old adage about not telling a lie because it is easier to remember and keep straight the truth is true. The dishonest and the deceitful always run the risk of being exposed. They never know when they might be found out, and the suspense can be even more destructive than their sinful deeds.

Deceit and dishonesty can be either willful duplicity or merely going along with someone else's dishonesty. Most of us find ourselves involved in the latter. For example, we let others get away with their questionable or even outright evil deeds and say nothing. When we can do something about a wrongful situation and do nothing, we share in the guilt of the wicked. Or when leaders abuse their power, the average person soon tries to see how much he or she can also get away with. We reason that since everyone else is doing it, we might as well join in. But we know better, and our lives become lies.

Integrity is a precious jewel with many facets. More than just not lying, it touches every part of our character and every aspect of life. For example, it does not rejoice when enemies stumble or fall (Prov. 24:17, 18).[18] Whybray sees the enemy here as a personal one and not some abstract opponent of God's people. It is not a struggle between good and bad people in which the Lord automatically sides with the good person. Rather, it is one of those petty human feuds that all of us find ourselves in. And God is partial to the underdogs in such disputes.[19]

We should not gloat over the fate of others, even our worst enemies. Even pagans have recognized this. The Mesopotamian wisdom teaching *The Words of Ahiqar* warned against rejoicing over an enemy's adversity.[20] The apostle Paul echoed a similar theme in Romans 11:18-21. The person of integrity will share God's sorrow that the situation has come to the point that one of His children must be punished and suffer.

The Motivation for Integrity

Non-Israelite wisdom teaching tended to look at what one did from the perspective of personal advantage. Its followers did this or that because it would help them succeed in life. But Israelite wisdom taught that we should do certain things simply because it was the right thing to do. The righteous lived a certain way because it was part of their transformed nature. What they did no longer rose out of a desire for gain or success. For example, they took good care of their animals (Prov. 12:10), not just so that their flocks and beasts of burden would produce more meat or wool or would work harder, but because their owners reflected the same kind of care for nature that God had for His human creation. They would no more be cruel to an animal than they would be to a family member. Such concern for the animal's "needs and desires and quirks" is a matter "not merely of profit (cf. 27:23, 29), but of virtue, and the wicked lack this ability."[21]

On a human level, kindness to animals reproduced God's attention and love for all His creation, as we see, for example, commanded in Deuteronomy 25:4: "You shall not muzzle an ox while it is treading out the grain." Despite Paul's homiletic use of the passage in the New Testament as an argument for supporting church employees, it means here that the ox has the right to eat whatever it wants as it pulls a threshing sled over the mounds of grain. The hardworking animal has a right to an immediate share of the harvest. It does not have to wait until its owner decides to feed it. By the same argument, human beings must not selfishly hoard the grain for themselves.

God cares for His creation, and the human race should manifest that same devotion in all its relations with other living things. The Creator is never self-centered, and neither should be any part of His creation—especially the men and women God appointed to be its stewards (Gen. 1:26). Integrity always operates on that same love for others that motivates God Himself.

The integrity that divine wisdom offers is not a destination but a journey. Those who seek wisdom can never announce one day that they have reached ultimate perfection and righteousness. The fact that they would even make such a claim would show how little growth they had actually made. David and other Old Testament individuals might speak of themselves as righteousness, but it was a maturing and relative thing, not an absolute righteousness. The sage declares that "the path of the righteous is like the light of dawn, which shines brighter and brighter until full day" (Prov. 4:18).

The ancients had only tiny oil lamps that would fit into the palm of their hand. Nighttime was extremely dark, unlike the modern world in which streetlights and the glow of all-night convenience stores and other buildings obscure the stars. Thus dawn was a powerful metaphor in the biblical world. It burned away the darkness as it rose from behind the hills, drying up the shadows like dwindling pools of water until they vanished. Daylight would first reveal shapes and outlines, then details. Wisdom did that in life, first showing the outline of God's plan for our lives, then filling in more and more of the details. It never revealed all knowledge immediately. The journey of understanding took a lifetime. The sage of Proverbs may have thought that one could acquire the fullness of wisdom in this life if a person lived long enough, but the continuing revelation of Scripture hints that wisdom is as infinite as its Creator.

And finally, integrity not only benefits the person who has it—but also it blesses others. "The righteous walk in integrity— happy are the children who follow them!" (Prov. 20:7). The people of the Bible recognized that divine blessing or punishment passed down to succeeding generations. God proclaimed the principle in Exodus 20:4-6. Family studies have revealed that both good traits—and, sadly, more often dysfunctional ones— can pass down the family line. Bad parenting and poor ways of coping get transmitted from adult to child and can continue in an unending cycle unless broken by some form of intervention.

Even the Bible shows, for example, in the story of Laban and his daughters, this unfortunate principle in operation. It demonstrates how parents who manipulate their children and treat them as objects train the next generation to do the same. Laban used his daughters as bargaining chips to control Jacob. They in turn used their female servants as devices to gain their husband's love. Both father and daughters treated others as objects to achieve their own purposes. The bad can pass from generation to generation—but so can the blessing of integrity.

Parents can give their children no greater inheritance than to lead lives of integrity. They will be powerful role models, teaching them by example true wisdom and righteousness.[22] Nothing will provide for our children more than for us to find true wisdom and live in the fear of the Lord.

---

[1] Joyce Tyldesley, *Daughters of Isis: Women of Ancient Egypt,* pp. 248, 249.

[2] Roland E. Murphy, *Proverbs,* p. 16.

[3] Derek Kidner, *Proverbs,* p. 61.

[4] In a world in which paths never went more than a short distance before having to detour up or around some obstacle, the imagery of a straight path would have been a symbol of great power on God's part. Only He could enable them to overcome the constant obstacles in the way while maintaining a straight path.

[5] Whybray observes that since almost all the Hebrew manuscripts of Proverbs have the reading "when a wicked man dies," it "might imply that for the righteous man there is a life after death, a doctrine otherwise unknown to Proverbs" (R. N. Whybray, *The Book of Proverbs,* p. 67). The Hebrew of Proverbs 14:32 might also give a hint that death is not the end. See Kidner (pp. 53-56) for a discussion on life and death in Proverbs.

[6] Whybray, p. 117.

[7] Murphy, *Proverbs,* p. 122.

[8] *Ibid.,* p. 222.

[9] *Ibid.,* p. 241.

[10] The term literally means "divination," and is "an expression for the finality with which this man speaks" (Kidner, p. 119).

[11] Lifting up the eyes can be positive or negative. For the former, cf. such passages as Psalm 123:1, 2, in which God's followers look to Him for favor.

[12] Murphy, *Proverbs,* p. 135.

[13] Whybray, p. 104.

[14] *Ibid.,* p. 143.

[15] R.B.Y. Scott, *Proverbs/Ecclesiastes,* p. 122.

[16] Whybray suggests that the phrase about hating one's own life may mean that such persons not only harm themselves, but also wished they were dead since they will constantly fear that the curse in the latter part of the verse may strike at any moment (Whybray, p. 169).

[17] Murphy, *Proverbs,* p. 223.

[18] Verse 18 is a puzzling one. Does it mean that the Lord considers such vengeful feelings as evil and will halt His divine wrath against our opponent? Or are we to suppress our pleasure at seeing what is happening to the enemy to ensure that the punishment will continue? Could it be that our reaction so displeases God that He will turn His attention on us? Murphy wonders if the saying is deliberately ambiguous to present several meanings (*ibid.,* p. 182).

[19] Whybray, p. 140.

[20] D. Winton Thomas, ed., *Documents From Old Testament Times,* p. 271.

[21] Murphy, *Proverbs,* p. 90.

[22] Kidner sees Proverbs 20:7 as also answering "the temptation to 'get on' at all costs 'for the children's sake'" (p. 137).

Chapter Eight

THE PATH TO POWERFUL WORDS

Unlike modern cynics who mutter that words are cheap, the ancients found them fascinating and even considered them powerful. After all, words could lead to life or death, healing or hurt. Also words brought joy, started or stopped great projects, and controlled almost every aspect of life. Words were the primary form of communication, a divine gift. The Egyptians even referred to their hieroglyphs as *medu netcher,* "the god's words."

The ancients even saw words as creative. The Egyptian god Ptah[1] brought the other gods and such things as life, food, and justice into existence. One ancient text described Ptah as "the mouth which pronounced the name of everything."[2] His creative words were "what the head thought and the tongue commanded."[3] Ptah would think of something, and his words would bring it into existence.

And, of course, the greatest example of creation by word appears in Genesis 1.[4] God speaks and both living and nonliving things come into being. While the passage does not mention the heart of God, it does refer to His Spirit (Gen. 1:2), sometimes translated "wind," as in the New Revised Standard Version. The imagery of the heart, the tongue, and in Genesis the hovering Spirit, belonged to a widespread way of describing the human personality. The Mediterranean world divided the human personality into three parts or zones:

1. The zone of emotion/thought.[5] The first zone included such areas as intellect, judgment, personality, and feeling. The ancients symbolized it by the eyes and heart. A person sees, thinks, understands, loves, makes decisions, and does other reason-oriented functions.

2. The zone of communication and self-expression. It included listening and responding, and the ancients presented it through the imagery of the mouth, ears, tongue, lips, throat, and teeth. People heard and did all verbal activity with the aid of this zone.

3. The zone of conscious action in which beings interact with the world around them. Mediterraneans depicted it through what the hands, feet, fingers, and feet did. Human beings did everything involving physical activity through this zone.[6]

Words are important to the book of Proverbs because they reveal what is in a person's heart, or personality. They reveal who he or she really is. In turn, words have a powerful impact on others, transforming them for better or worse. Our words can affect thoughts, actions, and character. In sum, they can influence everything. Proverbs 6:16-19 lists seven things that God hates or considers an abomination. Many of them involve the misuse of words, especially the "lying tongue" (verse 17), "a lying witness" (verse 19), and those who sow family discord, probably through what they say (verse 19).

We will look at how Proverbs evaluates words.[7]

What Words Can Do

The sage observes that "death and life are in the power of the tongue" (Prov. 18:21). What we say (and, by implication, think) can lead either to life or death both for ourselves and others. Words manifest their potential in several ways.

1. Words have effects, especially on the inner being, the personality. They always exist in a social context and have emo-

tional overtones. Our words are the main way we have of communicating what is important to us, whether it be relationships, ideas, values, fears and dreams, or anything else in life.

Rising from all that we are or do, words can hurt or strengthen these things. Thus, for example, they can injure our feelings. Rash words can cut like sword thrusts, while wise ones can bring emotional healing (Prov. 12:18). What the righteous say can feed us spiritually (Prov. 10:21). On the other hand, words from the wicked can devastate us. A good word can cheer up the anxious heart (Prov. 12:25). In fact, not only do they satisfy the soul like wild honey in a world that did not yet know sugar, but words also invigorate us physically (Prov. 16:24). "Good news refreshes the body" (Prov. 15:30).

On the other hand, words can be destructive. Gossip and slander can be as addictive as any drug. Rumors can be "like delicious morsels" swallowed and digested until they become a part of us—to our own detriment (Prov. 18:8). Both lies and flattery can destroy (Prov. 26:28; Prov. 11:9). The text is unclear whether it is the one who hates or the target of that hate who gets hurt,[8] but experience teaches us that gossip and slander can injure both. Whispering campaigns can wreck even the closest of friendships (Prov. 16:28). Flattery inflates the ego of the recipient, while the person who dispenses it sells out his or her integrity.

2. The effect of words, whether for good or bad, when once started cannot be halted. The almost unstoppable consequences of malicious words is the most obvious. They burn others like a scorching fire (Prov. 16:27). Perhaps the proverb has in mind flames racing through dry stubble or brush. The ancients had nothing for putting out such fires except beating them with their cloaks, which might only fan the flames. A similar thing happens with burning words. The more we try to stop slander or gossip, the more we seem to increase its spread. To deny an accusation only makes it appear more credible. Evil people through innuendo and "crooked speech" sow discord (Prov. 6:12-14). Winking (Prov. 6:13; 10:10; and 16:30)—not in a flir-

tatious sense—can be just as insidious and destructive as actual words. Ridicule, whether spoken or not, can ruin lives and reputations as effectively as outright lies. Perverse words can break another person's spirit (Prov. 15:4).

On the other hand, "a gentle tongue" is a tree of life (Prov. 15:4) or a fountain of life (Prov. 10:11). Both images are powerful biblical symbols often used to allude to eternal life, either that lost at the beginning or to be restored at the end.

What Words Cannot Do

1. Words can never substitute for action, a fact often forgotten by politicians immediately after the campaign ends. "In all toil there is profit, but mere talk leads only to poverty" (Prov. 14:23). Committees can discuss something forever, but unless someone puts plans into action, nothing will ever get done. Many cultures like to debate things, but only those civilizations that have tried to make their ideas work have changed history.

2. Public relations releases to the contrary, words do not change facts. A child may try to argue that he or she didn't break the vase, but the shattered fragments of pottery indicate otherwise. The media bombard us with words that seem to mean one thing but are really saying something else. Euphemisms may do more than simply seek to soften harsh facts—they may attempt to deny them altogether. An automobile crash or a person's body smashing into something becomes "sudden deceleration syndrome." Think, for example, of the many ways we have of avoiding saying that a person is dead. He has "passed on," "is no longer with us," or is "resting." Some of these expressions almost deny the reality of the person's death.

An enemy may seek to deceive us with polished and gracious words (Prov. 26:25) or hide hate with guile (verse 26), but time and events will expose what they are really like (verses 26, 27). In the end, God will reveal the truthfulness of all words as He repays "all according to their deeds" (Prov. 24:12). The Lord who keeps watch over us all knows all.

3. As any parent trying to talk a child into doing or not doing something knows, words can't force anyone to do or be what they don't want to. "By mere words servants are not disciplined, for though they understand, they will not give heed" (Prov. 29:19).[9] People can choose to ignore us. They must decide for themselves whether or not they will respond. Only then will our words have any positive results.

The book of Proverbs urges its readers to search for their own wisdom and not passively echo what others think. Only we can make wisdom a part of our life and personality. "If you indeed cry out for insight, and raise your voice for understanding; if you seek it like silver, and search for it as hidden treasures—then you will understand the fear of the Lord and find the knowledge of God" (Prov. 2:3-5). Only then will the words of wisdom really transform us.

We must want to learn before others can teach us, no matter how blunt or forceful they might be. "A rebuke strikes deeper into a discerning person than a hundred blows into a fool" (Prov. 17:10).

But just as you cannot make someone do good against his or her will, so no one can force us to do evil if we chose not to. Slander and gossip, for example, can distort another's reputation with us only if we decide to listen to and believe what we hear or read. "An evildoer listens to wicked lips; and a liar gives heed to a mischievous tongue" (Prov. 17:4). The choice is ours. If we will to do evil, then we will latch on to every disreputable thing we hear. But if we elect to let the fear of the Lord guide our lives, we will ignore even the most hateful words.

Choice Words

The book of Proverbs seeks to teach us both what good words should be like and how we can then make them ourselves.

1. Perhaps because Middle Eastern cultures have been given to much exaggeration, deliberate falsehood, and misrepresentation, the biblical sage calls for honesty in words. "Righteous lips

are the delight of a king, and he loves those who speak what is right" (Prov. 16:13). Honesty would have been a rare thing in the ancient palace as courtiers lied and backstabbed in their jockeying for prestige and power. Modern ruling bodies do not seem to have improved much.

And honesty in a judicial situation is always a major concern. Proverbs 24:24 decries those who call the guilty innocent, and verse 26 exclaims over those who give an honest answer. "A faithful witness does not lie, but a false witness breathes out lies" (Prov. 14:5). With only limited physical evidence available in both criminal and civil cases, biblical justice was always concerned about perjury. Legal proceedings required more than one witness to convict (Deut. 17:6; 19:15), and the witness had to be the first to begin the execution (Deut. 17:7) in an attempt to circumvent the problem of dishonest witnesses. If we have to kill another person ourselves, hopefully most of us would hesitate before lying against someone. False witnesses would receive the punishment they were trying to bring upon their innocent victims (Deut. 19:16-20) as a warning to others. Exodus 20:16 specifically forbids bearing false witness, or perjury.

A truthful witness can save a life, but a lying one betrays justice (Prov. 14:25). Although we cannot see it in this life, ultimately perjurers and liars will receive their just punishment (Prov. 19:5).

Slander, gossip, and perjury are social problems or illnesses. They hurt not only individuals but groups and communities as well. When anything destroys a person's reputation or position, it affects all those in relationship to him or her. It raises questions about the honor and credibility of the group the slandered person belongs to. Rumors may divide families, institutions, churches, or communities into hostile factions distrustful of each other. Physical violence can break out. Gossip and slander are as infectious as any disease germs, and both people and groups need healing after such injurious words have torn apart or alienated relationships. Both victims and perpetrators need reconciliation and restoration to the community. Whereas words can cause social illness, the right words under the influence of the Holy Spirit can help heal those problems.

Dishonest words can take forms other than obvious lies. Many of us have been frustrated by people who complain that we have dealt unfairly with them in business or other situations, but inside they were gloating over how they had actually gotten the better part of the deal (Prov. 20:14). We also dislike those who play practical jokes or act recklessly, and their words and deeds can lead to unexpected consequences (Prov. 26:18, 19).

People naturally prefer to hear flattery rather than honesty, and many times it seems safer to tell people what they want to hear rather than what they need to hear, especially when they have a problem. But in the long run it is better for all involved to be honest (Prov. 27:5, 6). Flattery merely aids others in their self-destruction, and refusing to comment on a problem only allows the person to remain in denial. Eventually we will have to face responsibility for aiding others to persist in their refusal to face reality. But if the others will only stop and think about it, they might realize that the best thing we can do for them is to be honest and confront them with the facts of their problem (Prov. 28:23). If they are willing to listen, they will come to recognize that an honest rebuke is actually a most valuable gift (Prov. 25:12; cf. Prov. 19:25).

2. Anyone who has had to suffer through flowery and meaningless speeches will realize that the best words are often the fewest. However, we have no monopoly on verbosity. In the ancient Near East, for instance, even an oral greeting or salutation could mean a long, involved avalanche of words. "Eastern salutations can be elaborate and time-consuming."[10] Even today in some Eastern countries "greetings take a notoriously long time [as in] Zarma; or in Shona."[11] Perhaps that is why Jesus instructed His disciples to avoid greeting people (Luke 10:4).

The world so bombards us with words today that we can heartily agree with the biblical sage when he declares that "even fools who keep silent are considered wise; when they close their lips, they are deemed intelligent" (Prov. 17:28). What we hear on televised sound bites and during political and ceremonial speeches sadly convinces us that there are a whole lot of fools talking out there.

The sheer volume of words today devalues them. We have learned to tune them out in sheer self-defense. More people, whether public figures or otherwise, have gotten themselves into trouble by what they say than perhaps by any other means. It is not a new problem (Prov. 10:14; 13:3). Too few have yet discovered that the best way to preserve a friendship or any other relationship is to keep one's mouth shut (Prov. 11:12, 13).

3. Contrary to the demagogues, good words are calm ones. Proverbs 17:27 parallels the "knowledgeable" person of few words with the individual "cool in spirit"—someone of understanding.[12] "Those who are hot-tempered stir up strife, but those who are slow to anger calm contention" (Prov. 15:18).

People with a temper most often resort to words to vent their anger and frustration. Proverbs 14:29 equates being slow to anger with great intelligence or understanding, and a quick temper with folly. Proverbs 13:3 tells us to guard our mouths, to watch and even censor what we say.[13]

The book of Proverbs praises calmness for several reasons. It gives time to study an issue or problem so that we won't jump to conclusions. "The one who first states a case seems right, until the other comes and cross-examines" (Prov. 18:17). To leap to a conclusion before even hearing the issues involved is a shameful example of folly (verse 13). Life is one unending illustration of the near impossibility of getting across an idea or perspective to a close-minded and prejudiced world. Those who seek spiritual truth especially should hear all the evidence. Anyone who keeps hiding behind tradition or preconceived ideas will not learn.

Approaching a discussion or controversy in a calm manner allows tempers to cool and emotions to subside. While harsh, emotionally laden statements intensify hostility and other negative feelings, "a soft answer" has a calming influence (Prov. 15:1). It does not antagonize or back people into argumentative corners. Almost nothing can stop an argument quicker than the refusal to fight back.

But "with patience a ruler may be persuaded, and a soft tongue can break bones" (Prov. 25:15; cf. Prov. 16:14, 32). Not only can persistence change minds, but also the very act of remaining calm can pacify others. A quiet approach frees the other person from feeling they have to defend themselves and their positions, allowing them to hear what you have to say and to have time to consider it in nonthreatening ways. People do not want to be forced to change their mind, but if you calmly present your evidence, it will give the Holy Spirit an opportunity to help them evaluate what you say. A calm presentation also gives credibility to your position. Since you don't have to fight to defend it, it must have greater evidence and authority on its side.

4. Good words should always be appropriate to the situation, never nonsensical or irrelevant. The ancients delighted as much in a well-crafted phrase as moderns do in a well-designed car or computer system. They enjoyed using their God-implanted sense of creativity working with words just as we like to craft material things. Conversation, discussion, and debate were actual art forms.

"To make an apt answer is a joy to anyone, and a word in season, how good it is!" (Prov. 15:23). Notice that the biblical writer not only emphasizes how something is said, but also when. "Not only the content, but the timing is also important. Obviously good advice and good timing do not always coincide, especially in the delicate cases of human existence. One of the ideals of the sage was to have the right word at the right time, as this verse indicates; see 10:11a and also 15:1."[14]

Other wisdom teachers also recognized that we need to know when and where not to say something. *The Teaching of*

Ankhsheshonq, a document from late Egyptian history, urges its readers, "Do not say something when it is not the time for it." [15]

The love of well-chosen words also appears in such sayings as "the tongue of the righteous is choice silver" (Prov. 10:20), [16] "a word fitly spoken is like apples of gold in a setting of silver" (Prov. 25:11), and "like a gold ring or an ornament of gold is a wise rebuke to a listening ear" (verse 12). The sage compared "pleasant words" to a honeycomb (Prov. 16:24), one of the few sweeteners available before the discovery of cane sugar in the New World. Such words will give the recipient joy and health. Those who have the fear of the Lord will seek the guidance of the Holy Spirit to know when to press an issue and when to remain silent. The righteous will sense what is the best thing to say (Prov. 10:32).

Making Good Words

As all of us realize after saying the wrong thing at the wrong time, it is not easy to speak good words. It requires carefulness and thought on our part. The book of Proverbs teaches us how to make our words better.

Good words do not come spontaneously. They require effort and preparation. "The mind of the righteous ponders how to answer" (Prov. 15:28). We must think before we speak, unlike the wicked and foolish who utter the first thing that pops into their minds (verse 28; cf. verse 2). We must "guard" (Prov. 13:3) and "watch" (Prov. 21:23) what we say. Our words must be the product of careful reflection, not an instant reaction. Such thought requires putting into practice all that we have learned of true wisdom. Good words are a manifestation of the fear of the Lord in our lives.

The book of Proverbs reminds us that what we say stems from what we are. Our words reflect our inner character. The way we walk through life establishes the direction of our words. The tongue tells others the nature of our heart. Thus the biblical sage urges, "Keep your heart with all vigilance, for from it flow the springs of life" (Prov. 4:23). "In Near Eastern (and Israelite) thought, . . . the heart was the equivalent of what *we* call the head! *Guard your heart* means 'be ruled at all times by your intelligence rather than by your emotions.' Since the heart was to be the seat of the intelligence and also of the will, the control of it was more important than anything else."[17]

Because the tongue mirrors the heart, to have good words we must first have a good heart. As Jesus observed, "out of the abundance of the heart the mouth speaks" (Matt. 12:34). Only the lips of the righteous will know what is acceptable to say (Prov. 10:32). Only the wise can spread true knowledge (Prov. 15:7; 10:31). This applies to groups—families, nations, and churches—as well as to individuals.

Words are powerful, but they will destroy unless God is behind them. Good words come from a good person, and a good person is God's doing alone.

---

[1] The Egyptians considered him the creator god as early as the Old Kingdom (2686-2181 B.C.). See Ian Shaw and Paul Nicholson, *Dictionary of Ancient Egypt* (New York: Harry N. Abrams, 1995), p. 230.

[2] Siegfried Morenz, *Egyptian Religion,* trans. Anne E. Keep (Ithaca, N.Y.: Cornell University Press), p. 164.

[3] *Ibid.*

[4] A nineteenth-century religious writer became fascinated with reports of people speaking into a device that allowed sounds to vibrate a rubber diaphragm covered with powder. The vibrations formed patterns in the powder. Occasionally the patterns resembled the object represented by the word spoken into the apparatus. The word "tree" might form a treelike image. Although the author did not give it as an example of how God spoke the world and living things into existence, he did suggest that human beings had only the "forms" of living things in their breath, but "in the breath of God there are not only the forms, but the very living things themselves" (E. J. Waggoner, *The Gospel in Creation* [Battle Creek, Mich.: Review and Herald Pub. Assn., 1894], p. 24). Scripture does not mean that God's words had some inherent power, but that God brought His thoughts into concrete reality. As we shall see, speaking is one of the images that Scripture uses to tell us about God as a person.

[5] The ancients did not separate reasoning from emotions in the way moderns do.

[6] Bruce J. Malina and Richard L. Rohrbaugh, *Social-Science Commentary*

on the Synoptic Gospels, p. 56. This way of describing the human personality, besides helping us better understand what the Bible is saying, has theological implications as well. Interestingly, Scripture consistently portrays God the Father with imagery from zone 1, the Son with imagery from zone 2, and the Spirit with imagery from zone 3. When speaking of God in general, the Bible mingles imagery from all three zones. It is a subtle way of depicting the members of the Godhead as comprising one whole, single, and unified personality. The three members of the Godhead form one God.

[7] The scheme presented builds upon and elaborates the discussion by Derek Kidner, *Proverbs,* pp. 46-49.

[8] Roland E. Murphy, *Proverbs,* p. 203.

[9] Although most ancient readers would understand the verse to imply the necessity of physically beating a slave into subservience, the principle remains that words alone do not always suffice to change behavior.

[10] Leon Morris, *Luke,* Tyndale New Testament Commentaries (Grand Rapids: William B. Eerdmans Pub. Co., 1974, 1984), p. 182.

[11] J. Reiling and J. L. Swellengrebel, *A Handbook on the Gospel of Luke* (New York: United Bible Societies, 1971), p. 403.

[12] Egyptian wisdom writings also contrast the "hothead," whose lack of self-control leads to disaster, with the "silent man" who has mastered himself (for example, in the *Instruction of Amenemope). The Song of Antef* has a related concept of the "cool man" (R. N. Whybray, *The Book of Proverbs,* p. 102).

[13] Ancient Near Eastern wisdom often emphasized guarding the mouth. The Babylonian *Counsels of Wisdom* said: "Let your mouth be controlled and your speech guarded," and the *Teaching of Ahiqar* urged, "Guard your mouth more carefully than anything else" (cited in Whybray, p. 33). James 3:3-12 expands this theme in the New Testament.

[14] Murphy, *Proverbs,* p. 114.

[15] Miriam Lichtheim, *Ancient Egyptian Literature* (Berkeley, Calif.: University of California Press, 1980), Vol. III, p. 169.

[16] More than one proverb compares something to silver. Silver was more valuable than gold in ancient Egypt because the nation had lots of gold deposits but no silver mines. Palestine did have silver. Could the biblical writer have had an Egyptian form of these proverbs in mind?

[17] Whybray, *Proverbs,* p. 33.

Chapter Nine

WISDOM'S PATH IN CREATION

The biblical wisdom tradition had a strong interest in creation and the world God had made. The book of Job, another wisdom book, often discusses creation in both senses of the word, speaking of God's creative ability and using the things God created as illustrations for the various characters' arguments. In Job 38-41 the Lord emphasizes the infinite gulf between the patriarch's understanding and that of God by interrogating Job about the created world. God asks him if he can do various things in nature or even explain how the Creator does them. If the human patriarch cannot grasp the "simple" actions of God's creative work, how could he possibly understand why the Lord permits suffering (Job 40:6-9)?

The rest of the book also contains much creation imagery. In Job 3 the patriarch curses the day he was born by calling for a complete reversal of creation itself. Job 3:10 takes the imagery of Genesis 1 and turns it inside out. He pleads that there should no longer be light (verses 4-7), and next wants time abolished and, by implication, the heavenly bodies that God made to mark off time (verses 6, 9). Then he demands that the creatures of the sea cease to exist (verse 8). His curse employs images taken from the Creation story.[1]

Ecclesiastes and the Song of Solomon also incorporate

much creation imagery. But unlike moderns, who have grown up in a scientifically oriented world, the sages had comparatively little interest in how God made the universe or brought life into existence. God had made everything, but how He had done it was of minor importance. Nor were they even interested in what we would call scientific study—nature study for its own sake. Instead, Israel's wisdom teachers studied the world around them to discover God's ways and His expectations of how humanity should live. The natural world was "the showcase for divine activity. It is not contemplated in and for itself, but in relation to the creator."[2] Their interest in creation and the natural world focused on what it showed of God's dealings with His human creation. They searched nature for principles to guide human living. Nature's behavior would teach them how they as God's people should act. In many ways the sages regarded the natural world as a series of moral lessons.

Job summarizes wisdom's approach when he stated: "Ask the animals, and they will teach you; the birds of the air, and they will tell you; ask the plants of the earth, and they will teach you; and the fish of the sea will declare to you. Who among all these does not know that the hand of the Lord has done this?" (Job 12:7-9). Humanity needs to know what God does, because "in his hand is the life of every living thing and the breath of every human being" (verse 10). If we exist only because God sustains us, we must know how to live in ways that will please Him—ways that will follow the order He ordained for the universe He created.

God's Wisdom in Nature

In Proverbs 6:6-11 the sage tells the lazy people in his audience to learn a lesson from the lowly ant. Without having any ruler to prod it, the insect gathers food during the summer for the coming winter. The Israelite peasant could see its trails, often extending long distances from the threshing floors or other sources of seeds back to its underground nests. While most species of ants do not collect food for the winter—instead, searching all year round for food as they need it—several Palestinian varieties do store seeds.[3]

The sage then turns to the sluggard and demands, "How long will you lie there, O lazybones? When will you rise from your sleep? A little sleep, a little slumber, a little folding of the hands to rest, and poverty will come upon you like a robber, and want, like an armed warrior" (verses 9-11).

Wisdom literature was not interested in studying ant behavior to find out more about the life and habits of the creature, but what practical lessons one could gain from them. The biblical interest was didactic, not scientific. The biblical sage did not seek knowledge for its own sake, but for its practical value in daily life.

Proverbs 30:15 introduces a series of sayings about things "never satisfied" by using the illustration of a leech. "The leech has two daughters; 'Give, give,' they cry." Murphy comments that the leech has two suckers at each end of its body, which the parasite uses to draw blood until bloated. "These are the 'daughters,' just as branches are construed as 'daughters' of a tree in the difficult text of Genesis 49:22. They are further personified by the twofold imperative, asking for more blood until satisfaction is reached. . . . In the context of verses 15b, 16, these bloodsuckers are an appropriate introduction to the insatiability of the four things that are to be enumerated."[4]

Verses 18 and 19 list four phenomena beyond the sage's understanding. Two of them involve creatures in nature. The scribe cannot grasp how an eagle can fly or how a snake can move without legs. Murphy sees them as half of a series of things whose path or course is beyond recovery.[5]

Two more numerical series appear in verses 24-28 and 29-31. The first group of sayings recognizes that one can be small and apparently helpless but still wise. Verse 25 is another use of ant imagery. The creatures have no visible leadership—no bureaucracy like human society—but they can still plan ahead.

Perhaps the sage is implying that they follow God's order, unlike human beings.

The badger of verse 26 is probably the rock badger, or cony. Naturalists consider it a member of the hyrax family. It is a small ungulate mammal similar in size to a rabbit but more closely resembling a guinea pig. The Syrian hyrax (*Procavia capensis syriacus*) lives in many parts of Palestine, especially the Galilee region. The creatures make their homes among rock outcroppings. Their flat, bare-soled feet enable them to move safely across the slippery rock surfaces.[6] The sage visualizes them as living in impenetrable rock fortresses.

Locusts also swarm across the landscape without any apparent leadership (verse 27). Unlike a human army, they don't need a king or officers to drive them in their conquest. The insects show no fear, and nothing distracts them. They behave the way God made them. Again, perhaps the sage is suggesting that, better than human beings do, they follow the wisdom and order that God ordained.

Verse 28 considers the numerous small lizards that wander in their search for food even through palaces. While they might be weak and easily caught, they could still live in a royal palace. And although human beings might not be able to get past the guards and palace bureaucracy, the insignificant lizard has no such problems. It scuttles into a domain that others try to bribe their way into—and fail.

The final series offers examples of stateliness, including the lion and the goat. People knew these animals well. The lions of Palestine belonged to the Asiatic subspecies *Panthera leo persica*. At one time they ranged from Greece across Asia Minor, Syria, Mesopotamia, and into northwest India. They became extinct in Palestine by the end of the Crusades during the thirteenth century, though they survived in Syria until late into the nineteenth century.

Lions so impressed the people of the Bible that artisans used images of them in Solomon's palace (1 Kings 10:19ff.) as well as in the temple he built (1 Kings 7:29, 36). The book of Proverbs compares the wrath of a king to the roaring of the lions that they heard shattering the peace of the rocky Palestinian hills (Prov. 19:12).

The hardy goats managed to thrive in the semiarid land when sheep had a harder time finding vegetation. They pranced across the pastures and fields.

Scholars are not sure what the Hebrew term in the first part of verse 31 means, so some translations use a reading based on the Septuagint. The Greek translation renders the word as cock, or rooster, but chickens did not reach Palestine until later.

The graded series of illustrations concludes with a human king who, if he is wise, will be the most stately of all. If creatures that obey God's natural laws are magnificent, then more so, King Lemuel's mother declares, should be leaders who adhere to the divine order.

The book of Proverbs has less to say about the physical world than it does the biological. Proverbs 3:19, 20 simply states that God "by wisdom founded" the physical world and established the heavens. He created the sources of water, both in the ground and in the sky. The passage uses imagery understandable to the people of biblical times rather than modern scientific language. The statement that God created "by wisdom" (verse 19) opens up a theological dimension to the book's interest in creation. It was a theological exploration that would reach its climax in the New Testament and early church.

As we have seen previously, the book of Proverbs personifies wisdom as a woman throughout chapters 1-9. In chapter 8, Dame, or Lady, Wisdom speaks in the first person. Verses 22-31 focus on the relationship of wisdom to Creation.

Wisdom and Creation

The woman named Wisdom declares in verse 22 that the first creative act God ever did was to bring her into existence. She came into being before anything else in the universe, including both matter (verse 26) and order (verse 29), the latter being of special concern to wisdom literature. "There is a strong emphasis on her origins and age. She was begotten of the Lord, and before anything else in creation. The style is unusual in its constructions: four times the use of the preposition 'from' ('of old,' etc., in verses 22, 23), and five times the implication of 'not yet' ('when,' 'before,' in verses 24-26). These constructions underline Wisdom's origins before all else."[7]

The string of expressions emphasizing antiquity and the far distant past combine to stress the idea that she existed before all other things. The passage lists a collection of things that came after her: depths and springs of water (verse 24), mountains and hills (verse 25), soil (verse 26), the heavens (verse 27), the skies and fountains of the deep (verse 28), and the boundaries of the sea and the foundations of the earth (verse 29).

The description goes in ascending order in verses 24-27—from the depths to the heavens—then switches somewhat to a reverse order, perhaps forming a chiastic structure. All are allusions to the Creation account in Genesis and its amplification in Job and the psalms. And Wisdom is present when all this happens, standing beside God "like a master worker" (verse 30). (The Hebrew word here is 'amôn.)

Some see Wisdom in verse 30 as a craftsperson (based on the Septuagint, Peshitta, and Vulgate translations of the Hebrew) assisting God in Creation, or she is a "child" or "nursling" who "plays" before God.[8]

Wisdom rejoices before God always (verse 30), finding joy in the human race and delight[9] in the world it inhabits (verse 31). She plays[10] both before God and with human beings "almost as if these humans were fitting playmates. Is this a kind of paradise experience? It is hard to imagine a bolder claim: to operate joyfully both before God and before humans."[11]

The Mesopotamian creation stories have the higher gods creating human beings to do the work that the lesser gods refused to do. The human race was nothing more than servants—and unruly ones at that. But here we have God through Dame Wisdom interacting with humanity and finding great pleasure in them.

The passage, however, raises many questions. First, who is Dame Wisdom? Is she a hypostasis, that is, an attribute or activity of God endowed with a personal identity? Or is she a highly poetic personification? An abstraction given human characteristics? Kidner, who views her as a personification, argues that "not only does the next chapter [of Proverbs] proceed immediately to a fresh portrait of wisdom, in a new guise (as a great lady [9:1-6] whose rival [13-18] is certainly no hypostasis), but the present passage makes excellent sense at the level of metaphor: i.e., as a powerful way of saying that if we must do nothing without wisdom, God Himself has made and done nothing without it. The wisdom by which the world is rightly used is none other than the wisdom by which it exists."[12] Even God needs Wisdom. He cannot create without her.

Roland Murphy points out: "She seems to be something of God, born of God, in God."[13] And elsewhere he goes so far as to say: "She seems to be divine, but subject to the Lord whose delight she is. . . . I would suggest that she is a surrogate for YHWH."[14]

Whatever she might be, Dame Wisdom is clearly not a goddess like the Egyptian Maat or like Ishtar, the Babylonian "creatress of wisdom." The rest of the book reveals no trace of polytheistic belief,[15] so we should not expect to find any here. Nowhere does the Bible worship or pray to her. Proverbs uses Wisdom in chapter 8 as a literary device, whether it be a metaphor, personification, or something else. But the image in the book started a line of theological thought that would eventually lead to an understanding of Christ as fully God and a member of the Godhead, or as the Christian church came to call it, the Trinity.

The imagery of Wisdom influenced later wisdom books, particularly chapter 24 of Ecclesiasticus and chapters 7 and 8 of the Wisdom of Solomon.[16] (Both books form part of the Old Testament Apocrypha.) The two books helped elevate Wisdom in theological thought to the status of a distinct person, even though still subject to God. Eventually commentators identified Wisdom with the Law, the Word of God, and the Spirit of God.[17] The Jewish philosopher Philo said that "the universe was fabricated" by the Logos-Wisdom.[18]

The New Testament applied wisdom imagery to Jesus. Christ is "the wisdom of God" (1 Cor. 1:24).

"He is the image of the invisible God, the firstborn of all creation; for in him all things in heaven and on earth were created, things visible and invisible, whether thrones or dominions or rulers or powers—all things have been created through him and for him. He himself is before all things, and in him all things hold together" (Col. 1:15-17).

Hebrews 1:2 declares that Christ created the worlds. More than that, "he is the reflection of God's glory" (verse 3), echoing Wisdom of Solomon 7:26, which says of Dame Wisdom, "she is a reflection of eternal light, a spotless mirror of the working of God, and an image of his goodness" (RSV).

And John begins his gospel by stating that Christ "was in the beginning with God. All things came into being through him, and without him not one thing came into being" (John 1:2, 3). The Saviour was light (verses 4, 5), another image Wisdom of Solomon uses of Dame Wisdom.

As the early Christians struggled to grasp more fully who Jesus was, they found help in the imagery of Wisdom. Origen, for example, in his book *On First Principles* pointed to the wisdom imagery applied to Christ in the New Testament and compared it to Proverbs 8:22-25 and other passages in the Septuagint as well as the Wisdom of Solomon. He concluded that the "wisdom of God has her substance nowhere else but in him who is the beginning of all things."[19]

Church historian Robert L. Wilken observes that "the presence of passages in the Septuagint that spoke of Wisdom as a divine agent, indeed as the preeminent divine agent, helped Christians understand the language of the New Testament and gave them an initial conceptual framework to express, on the one hand, the belief that Christ is God, and on the other, that he is not simply a divine attribute or emanation, but had his own proper existence."[20]

If Christ is the Wisdom of Proverbs 8:22-31, was He then a created being as the Arians argued? The Hebrew word translated here into English as "created" *(qanah)* usually means to "acquire" or "possess what has been acquired."[21] Genesis 48:22 uses it to refer to land that Jacob passed along to Joseph, and Isaiah 1:3 uses it of the ownership of an animal. The same meaning seems intended in the other 12 appearances of the word in the book of Proverbs.

The translations of the Old Testament into Greek by Aquila, Symmachus, and Theodotion, the Syriac version by Paul of Tella, and the Latin Vulgate all render *qanah* by words meaning "acquire" or "get." But three other versions—the Septuagint, the Peshitta, and the Aramaic Targum—employ in Proverbs 8:22 the less common meaning of "create," which appears in Deuteronomy 32:6, Psalm 139:13, and possibly Genesis 14:19 and 22. In Genesis 4:1 the word has an additional sense of "engender" or "give birth to." Because the Ugaritic Baal epic gives the goddess Athirat-Asherah the title "progenitress of the gods" *(qnyt'lm),* some commentators conclude the same meaning should be applied to the birth metaphor of Proverbs 8:24, 25.

But as we pointed out previously, the passage is saying that God's wisdom existed *before* He employed it to create anything. Thus R.B.Y. Scott concludes that the "meaning 'possess' for *qanah* is entirely suitable and is in keeping with the author's usage in 1:5, 4:5, 7. Yahweh 'possessed' wisdom as an asset or faculty integral to his being from the very first, and 'in [with, or by] his wisdom founded the earth' (3:19)."[22] Thus the emphasis is not on some hypothetical beginning of wisdom, but that God already had it before He started creating anything.

Instead of speculating on the origin of Christ, we need to focus on the point of Proverbs 8. Just as Wisdom "rejoiced" and "delighted" in God's creation, so we must be "happy" by listening[23] to the teacher of wisdom and incorporating that wisdom into all that we do and are (Prov. 8:32-34). To find wisdom brings life and favor (verse 35), but to neglect it leads to death (verse 36). The Christian would put it this way: to find Christ gives us eternal life and favor, but to ignore Him leads to eternal death.

---

[1] Older scholars tried to link Genesis and Job by appealing to certain obscure words and references to Egyptian culture that appeared only in the Pentateuch. But a stronger argument would be the many literary allusions, especially to the Creation story, that appear in Job.

[2] Roland E. Murphy, *The Tree of Life: An Exploration of Biblical Wisdom Literature* (New York: Doubleday, 1990), p. 119.

[3] *International Standard Bible Encyclopedia*, vol. 1, p. 129. Proverbs 30:25 makes a similar reference to the seed-gathering habit of the harvester ant.

[4] Murphy, *Proverbs*, p. 234.

[5] *Ibid.*, p. 235.

[6] *International Standard Bible Encyclopedia*, vol. 4, p. 206.

[7] Murphy, *Proverbs*, p. 52.

[8] See, for example, Derek Kidner, *Proverbs*, pp. 80, 81; Murphy, *Proverbs*, p. 53; R.B.Y. Scott, *Proverbs/Ecclesiastes*, p. 72; and R. N. Whybray, *The Book of Proverbs*, p. 52. Richard J. Clifford explores some of the ancient Near Eastern background suggested for the figure of Dame Wisdom (*Proverbs*, pp. 23-28). He also discusses the meaning of *'amôn* on pp. 99-101.

[9] Kidner suggests that we could consider this as meaning "I was happiness itself" in her attitude toward the human race (p. 81).

[10] Whybray sees here a picture of a child playing by its father's side (p. 52).

[11] Murphy, *Proverbs*, p. 53.

[12] Kidner, pp. 78, 79.

[13] Roland E. Murphy, "Wisdom in the OT," *Anchor Bible Dictionary* (New York: Doubleday, 1992), vol. 6, p. 927.

[14] Murphy, *Proverbs*, p. 280.

[15] Scott, *Proverbs/Ecclesiastes*, p. 69.

[16] Wisdom is "the fashioner of all things" (Wisdom of Solomon 7:22, RSV) and "an associate in [God's] works" (Wisdom of Solomon 8:4, RSV). See Clifford, pp. 98, 99.

[17] Whybray, p. 51.

[18] Scott, p. 70.

[19] Cited in Robert L. Wilken, *Remembering the Christian Past* (Grand Rapids: Eerdmans, 1995), p. 70.

[20] *Ibid.*, p. 71.

[21] Scott, p. 71.

[22] *Ibid.*, p. 72.

[23] Listening in the book of Proverbs, as we saw earlier, is not a passive thing, but an active response to what one hears, a putting of it into practice.

Chapter Ten

THE PATH TO TRUE HAPPINESS

In this chapter we will look at the themes of happiness and anger in the book of Proverbs. As always, the biblical world would have seen both emotions within the context of a dyadic personality instead of a modern individualistic one. While the writer speaks to the implied individual reader, he is also addressing his community as a whole. We should try to discover how the biblical sage's advice on happiness and anger applies to the family, church, community, and any other group as well as the individual person. Our happiness and anger affect not just us, but all those around us. They can catch our joy or our rage. In addition, groups themselves can also be happy or angry, as we see in sports fans and rioting mobs.

A Cheerful Heart

Perhaps one of the most widely known proverbs—even among the biblically illiterate—is Proverbs 17:22: "A cheerful heart is a good medicine, but a downcast spirit dries up the bones." The saying has become a cliché. However, everyday experience, as well as modern scientific research, reminds us that our attitudes influence our physical health. Any strong emotion, whether it be grief, joy, anger, fear, or anything else, can trigger powerful responses in the body. Negative emotions put great stress on the body, especially on the immune and circulatory systems.

Recent studies, for example, by the American Diabetes Association and the American Sociological Association indicate that depression can worsen the effects of diabetes. The research suggests that biological and psychological factors—especially stress—affect how the body controls blood sugar levels. The author of the psychological study said: "It looks like improving mental health improves diabetes."[1] *USA Today June 21, 99.*

Lowered immunity can also lead to increased infections and greater risk of cancer and various degenerative diseases. Positive emotions strengthen the immune system, enabling it to resist disease. Joy and happiness reduce stress and the damage it causes.

Today it has become common to equate happiness and good health. But it took medical science a long time to recognize the role that emotions and thought play in bodily processes, what we call the unity of mind and body. The Bible clearly teaches the interrelationship of mind and body,[2] but the popular belief in a separate immortal soul discouraged physicians and other scientists from seeing any connection. Yet ordinary experience teaches us that a cold, an upset stomach, or a headache can affect our personality. We find it hard to think clearly or control our emotions when we have, for instance, a throbbing toothache. Fear or worry can produce nausea, diarrhea, hives, or any number of physical conditions.

Scientific research has shown that emotions alter the body's biochemistry and development. In turn, physical conditions in the body can change the biochemistry of the brain and influence how we think and feel. Once we recognize these kinds of relationships, we have greater control over our lives. By choosing wisely in anything that affects our emotions or our bodies, we can have happier, healthier lives.

Modern medicine is increasingly trying to prevent disease by recommending a healthy physical and emotional lifestyle. It

Diet
Exercise
Positive
Emotions

seeks to help people strengthen their bodies to resist stress and disease through diet, exercise, and positive emotions. As we feel better physically, our emotional state will improve, and that in turn will make us feel even healthier.

To a surprising extent we can choose whether we will be happy or not. A young mother had a problem with her daughter being cranky and irritable each morning. The woman struggled with the problem for a while, then had an idea. Each night before she put the child to bed, she told her, "You will wake up happy." Soon the child began to wake up in a good mood. The girl had decided she would be happy.

Even in situations beyond our control we still have the freedom to make a choice about how we will respond. We can wallow in misery and defeat, or we can take charge of as much of our lives as circumstances will allow, seeking positive choices whenever possible and refusing to give up in hopelessness. Studies of prisoners in concentration camps and of victims of various kinds of accidents and disasters have revealed that the major difference between those who perished and those who survived was that the latter refused to give up. Joy and willpower are powerful survival aids. And most important of all, we can put our lives in God's hands and trust Him to work things out for the best.

Proverbs 15:13 tells us that happiness naturally shows in the face while sorrow destroys the human spirit. Both emotions also reveal themselves in group behavior. We can quickly tell whether a group is joyful or depressed—sometimes more easily than we can with an individual.

Happiness can enable us to cope with problems that might otherwise overwhelm us. "All the days of the poor are hard, but a cheerful heart has a continual feast" (Prov. 15:15). At first glance the saying might seem contradictory. Roland Murphy suggests that "perhaps the generalization of verse 15b modifies the desperate situation found in verse 15a, in the sense that the afflicted can and must cultivate a happy heart.

Their lot is hard, but their internal attitude can help attain some joy in life."[3]

Such joy is not an escape into some fantasy world or a self-delusion, but rather a conscious decision. Opportunities to make a choice can be found in almost any situation. All of us have had our priorities suddenly changed by drastic circumstances. Something that we once dreaded might not seem so bad after all in contrast with a greater disaster. The poor who continually "feast" have learned to make a shift in priority and perspective through deliberate choice.

If we had to decide which had a more powerful impact on life—the mental/emotional factors or the physical ones—perhaps we might lean toward the former. "The human spirit will endure sickness; but a broken spirit—who can bear?" (Prov. 18:14). Many have overcome tremendous physical disability or sickness to lead happy lives, while others with perfect physical health have succumbed to emotional defeat. Suicide is the ultimate tragedy of a crushed spirit. Families and other groups have also triumphed over great adversity—or let it defeat them.

But we do not have to find happiness or struggle with problems on our own. We can help each other, sometimes through such a simple thing as encouragement. "Anxiety weighs down the human heart, but a good word cheers it up" (Prov. 12:25). Words, as we saw in chapter 8, can be powerful. Here "the 'good word' (literally, in line b) is spoken by one who brings some comfort to the afflicted. The trouble is not specified, but there is no question that the 'word' transforms the situation. There is perhaps an implicit recommendation to be cheerful oneself, and even to communicate that to others."[4]

[margin note: How we Help Others]

Strife

At the opposite pole to happiness we find such negative experiences and emotions as strife and anger. Nothing can destroy a community or even a whole society more surely than people who set out to stir up trouble and turmoil. Whether it be a tiny rural farm settlement or a teeming nation, anything that tears the threads that hold the social fabric together can rip the whole apart. If they don't immediately wreck the social fabric, they can weaken it and threaten its survival.

Proverbs 13:10 reminds us that an insolent or arrogant attitude can cause social dissension as does the person who delights in transgression (Prov. 17:19). Scoffing can disturb social harmony, causing quarreling and abuse (Prov. 22:10). It undermines authority and credibility. We have seen its power to destroy reputations in political contests and ideological disputes. If you can't defeat a person or concept on merit, turn the person or idea into a laughingstock.

Proverbs 26:21 compares a quarrelsome person to fuel that sets a fire blazing. An individual given to quarreling can turn the members of a family or committee against each other or otherwise drive them apart.

A common cause of social strife, especially in smaller, close-knit groups, is gossiping. A powerful force in family or community, it can be positive, providing a way to share information, release frustration, or offering social control by maintaining social values and the status quo. It forms and maintains the boundaries of social groups, and provides information on who is honest or not in business and other dealings.[5] The latter use was especially prominent in the small communities of the biblical world. Anyone who began to seek too much power or wealth or behaved in ways the community considered deviant and threatening could often be brought into line by gossip.[6] But, as we all know too well, gossiping is far more often destructive. It undermines reputations and turns people into enemies.

Plutarch wrote in the first century that "just as cooks pray for a good crop of young animals and fishermen for a good haul of fish, in the same way busybodies pray for a good crop of calamities, a good haul of difficulties, or novelties and changes, that they, like cooks and fishermen, may always have something to fish out or butcher." Gossips ignore the beautiful and worthwhile so that they can "spend their time digging into other men's trifling correspondence, gluing their ears to their neighbor's walls, whispering with slaves and women of the streets, and often incurring danger, and always infamy."[7]

Today gossip spreads not only by word of mouth, but also through the electronic media, especially via e-mail. Governments and other groups release disinformation—deliberately false or controversial information—to undermine their opponents. Once a rumor starts, it takes on a life of its own and may be impossible to kill while it destroys reputations and the credibility of both people and institutions.

Like a grass fire, the more one stomps on it, the more flames leap to start new fires. Recently certain prominent corporations involved in lawsuits have had to confront the rumors its employees started through e-mail and were preserved in electronic files that everybody thought had been erased. But if people refuse to pass rumors along, it will at least slow them down if not stop them altogether. Like fire that lacks fuel, quarreling will cease if people refrain from gossiping (Prov. 26:20).

Anger

Perhaps the most destructive emotion of all is anger.[8] It blinds us to reason and common sense. Quick-tempered people act foolishly (Prov. 14:17, 29). Fools leap into quarrels, while humble persons will avoid strife or do everything possible to defuse it (Prov. 20:3). Babylonian wisdom writing advises its audience that "when confronted with a dispute, go your way; pay no attention to it. Should it be a dispute of your own, extinguish the flame!"[9]

Some people seem driven to feed their own anger and stir up endless strife. What psychologists call rageaholics literally become addicted to the feelings and hormone levels of their own anger. It is as powerful as any other drug addiction. Most angry people are not rageaholics, but they can be even more destructive.

Through three vivid images Proverbs 30:33 suggests the violent results of clinging to anger. All three images contain the same verb, which can be translated "pressing." "For as pressing milk produces curds" captures the image of wringing a large animal-skin bottle full of milk hung from a tripod to process the milk into a form of butter.[10] The pressure in the second image causes a nosebleed, while pressure in the third image leads to anger. The sage in this passage utilizes a play on words, since the Hebrew words for "nose" and "anger" have a similar sound.[11] People have devastated reputations, lives, and even whole communities by pressing—never letting up on—their anger. Eventually they destroy themselves. The only way to avoid such disaster is to stop feeding such all-consuming rage.

It is much better to be slow in giving in to anger. Proverbs 16:32 says that those who have their anger under control are better than even powerful military leaders who can capture a heavily defended city. It takes great leadership skills and persistence to hold an army together long enough to starve out a population or break through the walls before disease spreads from overcrowding through your own military camp. Your troops, losing interest in the protracted siege, desert to go home so they can take care of their families, herds, and crops. You have to keep motivating them to endure the discomfort and outwait those inside the city you want to capture. Yet the Bible sees the person who can control his or her anger as even more powerful.

In the words of R. N. Whybray: "It is the patient administrator who gets to the top and stays there."[12] But those who lack self-control are like an unwalled city, defenseless against any attack of anger and passion (Prov. 25:28).

We have to be extremely careful in our dealings with those ruled by anger. If you try to rescue them from the unfortunate consequences of their latest explosion of rage, you have a good chance of becoming the target of that anger yourself. But more than that, you will have to do it again—and again (Prov. 19:19). They never learn. James 1:19, 20 takes up this theme in the New Testament. Anger only leads to more anger and totally dominates those who give in to their wrath. Such angry people become their own worst enemies, destroying their happiness and health and everyone and everything they love.

One of the most frequent causes of anger is our frustration when someone hurts or insults us or those whom we love. This was especially the case in the ancient world. People viewed everything through the perspective that it brought either honor or shame.[13] The obsession to protect one's honor often led to violence and blood feuds. Families and tribes slaughtered each other to protect or restore their honor.

Some of these ancient struggles still continue today, as we see ethnic groups fighting controversies that started many centuries ago. To those caught up in them some insult or dishonor that occurred in centuries past is as powerful as if it happened today. It was with good reason that the sage advised his readers, "Do not say, 'I will do to others as they have done to me; I will pay them back for what they have done'" (Prov. 24:29).

Why? Proverbs 20:22 tells us that it is God's responsibility to restore honor and bring vengeance, that we must "wait for the Lord, and he will help you." Centuries later Paul echoed Old Testament teaching when he declared: "Beloved, never avenge yourselves, but leave room for the wrath of God; for it is written, 'Vengeance is mine, I will repay, says the Lord'" (Rom. 12:19). God cannot intervene if we leave no room for His working but crowd Him out by trying to solve the problem ourselves—and in the process only making it worse. The apostle is merely summarizing teaching that appears in such passages as Deuteronomy 32:35, 41, 43; Leviticus 19:18; and Psalm 94:1. Old Testament prophets as well as Jesus Himself proclaimed the idea of God coming with vengeance to forever end injustice and dissension.

Anger and the desire for vengeance affect not only nations, but also families and even churches. Relatives don't speak to each other, and factions sit in their own particular sections of the church sanctuary or even split off into breakaway congregations. Only God can stop the cycle of pain and violence with justice that truly satisfies. And only He can give us happiness that is eternal and not fleeting. All who want to escape the prison of their anger and find true peace and joy must put all of life in His hands, His guidance.

[1] Anita Manning, "Depression Worsens Dangers of Diabetes," *USA Today,* June 21, 1999.

[2] I have discussed this in greater detail in my *Life Beyond Life: What the Bible Says About Life, Death, and Immortality.*

[3] Roland E. Murphy, *Proverbs,* p. 113.

[4] *Ibid.,* p. 92.

[5] Bruce J. Malina and Richard L. Rohrbaugh, *Social-Science Commentary on the Gospel of John,* p. 103.

[6] ——, *Social-Science Commentary on the Synoptic Gospels,* pp. 45, 185.

[7] Quoted in Malina and Rohrbaugh, p. 103.

[8] Anger under certain circumstances can be positive. It can motivate us to deal with abuse and injustice. Such emotion builds and resolves, not destroys. Jesus became angry at the moneychangers in the Temple, and Scripture often describes God as becoming angry at injustice and sin.

[9] D. Winton Thomas, *Documents From Old Testament Times,* p. 105.

[10] Derek Kidner, *Proverbs,* p.182.

[11] Murphy, *Proverbs,* p. 237; Kidner, p. 182; R. N. Whybray, *The Book of Proverbs,* p. 179.

[12] Whybray, p. 97.

[13] Malina and Rohrbaugh, *Synoptic Gospels,* pp. 76, 77, 213, 214, 309-311. Many Bible stories revolve around the theme of honor/shame or, in the case of Esther, their unexpected reversal.

Chapter Eleven

THE PATH TO TRUE FRIENDSHIP

People in the biblical world lived in houses clustered in small villages and towns. The typical Israelite home was what archaeologists refer to as the four-room house. Pillars and walls divided it into four areas. The family kept its cattle, donkeys, and other animals in one of the sections. The animals would provide a little warmth in the drafty dwelling during the cold months, but the smell would have been strong. People worked, cooked, and ate outside as much as possible and stayed inside primarily to sleep. They did not shut their doors during the day; society considered it suspect and abnormal behavior to do so.

Houses shared adjoining walls to save on building costs and space, thus voices carried easily from one building to another. The village would be noisy with the cries of animals, children playing, and men and women talking with great animation.[1] The air would reek with the stench of sewage, garbage, unwashed bodies, and cooking food.

Even the largest cities rarely covered more than a few acres. During most of its history Jerusalem, for example, was never more than 20 acres in size. Unlike the situation in modern urban areas, the rich lived in the center of the city and the poor along the walls, thus more exposed to crime or attack by besieging armies. The most poverty-stricken of all dwelled outside the city walls.

Farmers typically did not live on their land. It was too dangerous. They spent nights inside the village or town and went out to work their fields at dawn, returning before dark. If the town had gates—the difference between a village and a city was that the latter had defensive walls—the authorities would shut them at nightfall, locking everyone in for protection.

The people of the Bible rarely traveled. First, it was difficult because they had to go either on foot or donkey or ride in simple wooden-wheeled carts on rough, unpaved roads. Second, bandits lurked in the countryside. Apart from the very wealthy, no one ever went any distance for pleasure except during a few yearly religious festivals when the Israelites, particularly the men, journeyed to the sanctuary or Temple. Only war or plague would drive people elsewhere for any length of time.

They would never think of moving someplace else just to seek a better life. Palestine had no vast frontiers of fertile land to lure people. Every patch of ground capable of growing a crop or possessing a source of water was already occupied. Nor were there economic opportunities to beckon people to the cities. People were born, lived, and died in the same tiny area. They saw the same faces every day.

Because average Israelites lived with little or no privacy and could not move away if they alienated family or neighbors, they had no choice but to learn to get along with one another. Thus the book of Proverbs naturally has something to say about the necessity of friendship and what it takes to be a good friend.

The Biblical Definition of a Friend

Scripture regards friendship as more than just a casual association centered on shared interests or of belonging to some group. Nor was it based on nostalgia or shallow affection, as people today fondly remember schoolmates. Today we think of friendship as a purely personal choice. We select whom we would like to be friends with. In the ancient world, however, friendship was one of the core building blocks of society. It had survival value. People would have physically perished without friends. Friends are not only someone you liked to be with, but also they supported you during times of struggle and crisis.

"Friendship entails responsibilities and benefits. The proverb that 'a friend loves at all times' (Prov. 17:17) expresses both an obligation and a benefit. [Scripture, as we especially see in the New Testament, views love more as how we treat others than how we emotionally feel toward them. In the biblical world love meant what we would call loyalty.] In a similar vein is the proverb that 'there are friends who pretend to be friends, but there is a friend who sticks closer than a brother' (Prov. 18:24, RSV). In the Bible friendship is a mutual improvement activity, honing one for godly use. Biblical friendship is a face-to-face encounter, signifying proximity, intimate revelation and honesty. It is also a bonding of affections and trust, knitting one's very soul to another. In its ultimate reaches, it is union with God."[2] Good friendships will reflect on a human level the close relationship of the members of the Godhead. Being a friend means treating others as God would.

Friends always remain with us during both the good and bad times (Prov. 17:17). They not only give us companionship, but also counsel us—even when we may not want it. "Well meant are the wounds a friend inflicts, but profuse are the kisses of an enemy" (Prov. 27:6). They tell us what we *need* to hear, not just what we may *want* to hear. But false friends also exist. Thus Proverbs not only tells us what kind of people we should look for as friends, but what kind we should avoid. Let us look first at what Scripture regards as the joys of friendship.

The Joys of Friendship

Proverbs 27:10 observes that "better is a neighbor who is nearby than kindred who are far away," an observation which the Assyrian document *The Teachings of Ahiqar* also made.[3]

Although most people lived in extended families, perhaps occupying the same street or quarter of the city, nonrelated neighbors could also become like family. Being a neighbor was a fundamental social role with both privileges and obligations that came from simply living nearby others and being involved in their lives. It could involve belonging to the same village, neighborhood, or social group. Ancient Mediterranean society considered such groups as an extension of one's own kin group.

Malina and Rohrbaugh consider Proverbs 3:39; 6:29; 11:9, 12; 16:29; 25:9, 17, 28; 26:19; 27:10, 14; and 29:5 as illustrations of this principle.[4] Even in recent times people in Syria who lived at least 20 or more years in the same neighborhood came to consider themselves as cousins. Mediterranean society expected a person to defend such neighbors/friends with one's own life. Each individual must protect such "family" integrity as one would a close biological relative.[5] In the New Testament Jesus regarded the church and its members as family, one to replace those the believers might have lost when they became Christians.[6]

Fewer and fewer people in Western countries still know their neighbors, especially in apartment complexes. They rush off to their jobs and return home merely to sleep or catch a bit of television. Most know the people at work better than those across the hallway or street. Our work associates have become our modern neighbors and sometimes even a substitute family. Perhaps we have lost something in the process. But whoever and wherever our friends are, they can still be with us to help when even our family cannot. And with families in the developed world growing constantly smaller, friends become even more important.

As Proverbs 17:17 reminds us, "a friend loves at all times, and kinsfolk are born to share adversity." Although interpreters differ whether the passage contrasts friend and brother, or that a loyal friend actually becomes like a blood brother,[7] all would agree that we need the support, both emotional and physical, of those around us. Just as the ancients survived crises and disas-

ters only through the help of others, so we still need that support today. As members of the church we must see each other
as both neighbors and family. We must always be ready to love
and aid those cast off by their families because of their allegiance to Christ.

Friends are not only a source of help, but they can also be a
joy. They can make us more than we would ever be by ourselves. The New Revised Standard Version translates Proverbs
27:17: "Iron sharpens iron, and one person sharpens the wits
[or face] of another." The scribe has in mind the image of the
blacksmith honing the blade of a knife or hoe against an un-
worked piece of metal.

Roland Murphy states that while the Hebrew word "face"
has many potential meanings, including the concept "intelligence," "personality," and so forth, "at the very least, the saying
points to the beneficent personal effects that individuals can or
do have upon each other; no man is an island."[8]

Today the human race has almost become a maze of islands
lost in a sea of loneliness and despair. But in friendship each
person brings his or her unique strengths to others, compen-
sating both for their weaknesses and complementing or even
expanding beyond what they accomplish by themselves.
Friends nourish and multiply the best in others. They challenge
and stretch us.

How to Be a Friend

But, as the old adage goes, to have friends, we must ourselves be friends. Proverbs gives several suggestions for what
constitutes a friend. Proverbs 17:9 contrasts both what a friend
should do and what he or she must avoid. "One who forgives
an affront fosters friendship, but one who dwells on disputes
will alienate a friend."

In the confined world of the Israelite village, to nurse a
grudge or obsess on an insult would lead to an intolerable situation. There was no way to escape a neighbor. Today we might

be able to move physically halfway around the world, but even that does not really solve the problem. Our anger or hurt will travel with us. We have to forgive, or it will destroy us.

The best-known proverb about forgiveness has part of it quoted in the New Testament and has entered popular culture as a folk saying. "If your enemies are hungry, give them bread to eat; and if they are thirsty, give them water to drink; for you will heap coals of fire on their heads, and the Lord will reward you" (Prov. 25:21, 22).

Jesus expounds its general theme of doing good to those who hurt or persecute you as a means to overcome evil (Matt. 5:44; Luke 6:27). Paul not only cites the admonition to give food and drink to one's enemies, but also includes the enigmatic phrase about heaping "burning coals on their heads" (Rom. 12:20), urging his readers, "Do not be overcome by evil, but overcome evil with good" (verse 21).

The idea that a person should do good to an enemy is, of course, not a new one. The Egyptian *Instruction of Amenemope* from the New Kingdom counsels its readers to "fill his [the opponent's] belly with bread of your own, that he be sated and weep."[9] Treating our opponents with kindness can often make friends of them, or at least reduce their hostility. But what does it mean to "heap coals of fire" on someone?

Some of the explanations seem almost contradictory. Kidner suggests that the phrase stands for "the pangs which are far better felt now as shame than later as punishment."[10] One commentator sees it as a gift of actual coals that allow the enemy to easily ignite the household fire without having to go through the difficulty of starting it himself or herself. Others have conjectured that the image of coals originated in an ancient Egyptian repentance ritual[11] in which a person expiated wrongdoing by actually bearing coals on the head.[12]

But Roland Murphy rejects such an explanation, observing that "despite the verbal similarity, this Egyptian background has not been generally accepted; there is no evidence for such a rite in the Old Testament, nor is it clear how this rite would have found its way into Israel. Several other meanings have been proposed. The action is interpreted as producing punishment, or a burning shame, or remorse and conversion. Of these, the best understanding is that a change of heart on the part of the enemy is produced. Moreover, there is the assurance that the Lord will reward the person who acts with such magnanimity toward an enemy."[13]

Too often we have ignored the conclusion of the proverb "The Lord will reward you" (Prov. 25:22). As we saw earlier, many ancients tried to use the wisdom tradition as a device to guarantee success in life. The Egyptian scribes taught that if you followed their advice and did certain things, you would receive your reward. The proper etiquette automatically leads to it because that is the way the universe operates. Even the gods are bound by it. But biblical wisdom offers no such guarantee. You behave justly because God expects you to. He never promises an automatic reward. If any does come, it will be the Lord's doing—and His decision alone.

As we have seen, biblical wisdom presents a way of life that reflects that of the Creator Himself. While Scripture may present wisdom in terms of consequences—"If you close your ear to the cry of the poor, you will cry out and not be heard" (Prov. 21:13)—it seeks to lead men and women to do good to others whether or not they receive a reward in this life. While being charitable to others may make them more kindly disposed toward us, we should do it whether they reciprocate or not. We should follow the example of our Father in heaven who "sends rain on the righteous and on the unrighteous" (Matt. 5:45).[14]

God longs for His people to love others because they want to be like Him, not just to be a success in this life. That is what true friends are. They pattern themselves after the God of the universe.

---

[1] Notice the humorous truism in Proverbs 27:14: "Whoever blesses a neighbor with a loud voice, rising early in the morning, will be counted as cursing." Many people cannot cope with loud sounds in the morning.

[2] *Dictionary of Biblical Imagery*, p. 309.

[3] D. Winton Thomas, *Documents From Old Testament Times*, p. 273.

[4] Bruce J. Malina and Richard L. Rohrbaugh, *Social-Science Commentary on the Gospel of John*, p. 239.

[5] *Ibid.*, p. 235.

[6] ———, *Social-Science Commentary on the Synoptic Gospels*, pp. 99-101, 201, 202, 335, 336.

[7] Roland E. Murphy, *Proverbs*, pp. 130, 131.

[8] *Ibid.*, pp. 208, 209.

[9] Miriam Lichtheim, *Ancient Egyptian Literature*, Vol. II, p. 150. Matthews and Benjamin translate the last phrase of the Egyptian proverb as "until they are ashamed" (*Old Testament Parallels*, p. 191).

[10] Derek Kidner, *Proverbs*, p. 160.

[11] R.B.Y. Scott, *Proverbs/Ecclesiastes*, p. 156.

[12] Murphy, *Proverbs*, p. 193; Dictionary of Biblical Imagery, p. 739.

[13] Murphy, *Proverbs*, p. 193.

[14] The people of the biblical world considered rain one of the greatest of all blessings, since without it their crops would not grow and they would starve to death. Rain was not merely a nuisance that ruined a picnic or ball game.

Chapter Twelve

THE PATH TO A HAPPY MARRIAGE

Marriage in the biblical world was not just the romantic union found in modern societies in which the couple go off by themselves to live happily ever after. It was more a matter of economics than anything else. People married to ensure the survival of their family, tribe, or nation. Life was precarious in a world in which people were always just one harvest away from starvation. Marriage allowed families to pool their resources. The basic unit of all societies until recently was the extended family, not the so-called nuclear family. The latter is a modern invention made possible only by the Industrial Revolution. It cannot exist in a world that depends upon subsistence farming.

In the ancient world and even in some cultures today the whole family had to work together, tending crops and herds, cooking, making clothing and other household items, and coming to each other's aid in emergencies. The wife could not just stay home to tend the house. Everyone was needed. The more hands and backs to share the work, the better. People had to depend on their own efforts. If crops failed or disease or accidents struck, they turned to the extended family for help. No social service agencies or emergency relief organizations existed to tide them over a crisis. Only the network of relatives would get them through disaster. And the extended family included all those tied together through marriage.[1]

The economy has changed in the modern world, and it is possible for couples and even single persons to live by themselves. Recent surveys reveal that only one household out of every four consists of the "traditional" unit of parents with children. A growing percentage of households consist of a single person. Declining birth rates and people moving to distant cities to find work have destroyed the extended family to a large extent in the Western world, but it survives elsewhere in the world and among immigrants in Western countries. Modern men and women do not live as physically endangered lives as did the ancients, but they face just as serious dangers of other kinds. The stress of a fast-paced world, for example, threatens our physical and emotional health, and the extended family could help us cope with it. We could learn to build modern versions of the extended family from work, church, or other groups and find in them some of the strengths formerly provided by the extended biological family.

Finding Suitable Marriage Partners

When parents in the ancient Near East looked for marriage partners for their children, they would especially consider the resources of the prospective bride's or groom's extended family. The family of the potential son- or daughter-in-law had to be of a comparable economic level—neither poorer nor wealthier. To marry into a family with too great a difference in wealth could lead to constant tension or friction.

Society expected all to share their limited resources, to help out in daily life as well as emergencies, with the understanding that such assistance would be reciprocated by the receiving family as soon as the opportunity arose. Even wedding presents were considered a loan, and if something happened to the marriage, one could go to court to recover the gift.[2] A poor family could not provide what a wealthier family needed or expected. And a rich family might resent the normal demands put upon it by impoverished in-laws. Also the merged families would protect each other during war or from the depredations of bandits.

How many couples consider the economic, cultural, and social differences between their families before they marry? But tensions arising from those different backgrounds and circumstances will arise after the wedding, if not during it. Do engaged couples ever ask themselves if they can tolerate, let alone enjoy, intimate social contact with the members of each other's family? Even the members of today's fractured families do not live in isolation from each other. Modern couples could learn much from the way the ancients approached marriage.

Divorce Rarely an Option

The close and mandatory ties between in-laws meant that divorce was rare in the ancient world. One did not lightly risk losing the financial and labor support of a spouse's family. Nor did one want to alienate the spouse's family in the small, tightly knit villages of the biblical world. To cast a wife aside (in most cases only the husband had the right to divorce) not only insulted her family but dumped the responsibility of supporting her back on her relatives. Because divorce dishonored the woman's family, it could easily lead to a blood feud that could decimate entire families.[3] One dramatic example of the results of a divorce occurred when Herod Antipas divorced his first wife, the daughter of Aretas, king of the Nabateans. In retaliation her father attacked and conquered much of Antipas' territory east of the Jordan River.[4]

If a blood feud between families estranged by divorce did not immediately kill all the members, the strife could weaken either family to the point that some other crisis could then overwhelm it. Although it might seem that a man could divorce a wife on a whim in the biblical world, to actually do so had serious consequences. It probably happened rarely except among the wealthy.

Lost Resources

As we have pointed out, couples in modern Western societies do not always need the resources of the extended family to survive. (And the ancients would have been unable to imagine the idea of single individuals living by themselves.) The extended family was the primary economic, religious, educational, and social network.[5] But today's financial freedom for married couples often has come at a high price. They forget that when they wedded each other they also married into their spouse's family. Poor relations with in-laws can cripple, or even destroy, the marriage. In addition, as the modern couple live to themselves they neglect or lose the strengths and resources that only the extended family can provide. Whereas ancient families crowded together in tiny rooms, the members of modern Western families must cope with increasing isolation.

For example, as we alluded to earlier, until the middle of the twentieth century parents did not raise children by themselves. They had the help of grandparents, aunts and uncles, cousins, neighbors, and all the other people of a village or the immediate community. If communication broke down between mother and daughter, an aunt or other female relative could assure the girl that the mother didn't really mean to come across as judgmental in the way the daughter thought. And then the same family member could go to the mother and remind her how she had felt and reacted when she was her daughter's age. Neighbors used to keep an eye on local children and would caution them when they began to get involved in things the adults knew their parents would not approve of. In addition, neighbors provided role models and helped children acquire skills and knowledge that even their parents might not be able to teach.

When divorce strikes the modern nuclear family, it is especially devastating. Children lose the role models of two parents interacting with the children and with each other. Because mothers most frequently have primary custody, it deprives both boys and girls of the vital influence of a father. Divorce often plunges the ex-wife and the children into poverty. The fastest growing sector of people below the poverty line in North

America is children of divorce. It is difficult for a single parent—usually the mother—to support the family on one income or on limited child support as well as to provide the emotional needs usually given by two parents.

In addition, divorce frequently cuts grandparents and grandchildren off from each other. Even in intact nuclear families, children may not receive the emotional nourishing and role modeling that only older adults can supply. Retirement communities, large geographic distances between family members, and nursing homes also isolate the generations from each other.

The extended family cradled each member in a complex web of support and communication lacking in today's world of the so-called nuclear family. These ties strengthened people in a world of physical dangers, but are equally vital for survival from the psychological stresses of modern technological society. Although Scripture does not discuss the extended family directly, it shows through its many stories both its strengths and weaknesses. We find a few echoes of this even in the proverbs. To grasp fully the message of some of these proverbs we must place them within their cultural context of large interconnected families.

The people of the biblical world approached marriage in a way that recognized and preserved those ties and strengths. Although the book of Proverbs is not a marriage manual, it does contain a number of hints as to how to have a stronger marriage. Mostly they are observations that if placed in the framework of true wisdom will guide and protect the marriage institution. We must not project our modern Western families into Scripture or we may misinterpret what it has to say, but we can still learn much from what it teaches about marriage.

Marriage in the Biblical World

The biblical world to a large extent divided gender responsibilities between the home and public spheres.[6] Although both sexes would labor together in the field, women had charge of the home and children while men were most active in civic affairs. (As we shall see when we examine the "Ode to a Capable Wife" in Proverbs 31:10-31, though the boundaries were more fluid than we might expect. The people of the biblical world did not live like nineteenth-century Victorians, who treated women as helpless and passive.)

Because the book of Proverbs most likely originated in a male world, it reflects more of a male perspective than a feminine one. Thus it has more to say about the desired characteristics of wives than of husbands. But even then Proverbs recognizes the role the wife fulfills in making a marriage happy or frustrating. "He who finds a wife finds a good thing; and obtains favor from the Lord" (Prov. 18:22).

Kidner says the Hebrew of the verse "strikingly resembles that of [Prov.] 8:35, and so suggests that after wisdom itself, the best of God's blessings is a good wife."[7] Although we are again seeing through a male perspective, the biblical author recognizes "that the husband has little to do acquiring such a prize."[8]

How many modern couples see God playing any significant role in courtship and marriage or recognize that He is the key to a successful marriage? R.B.Y. Scott suggests that the Hebrew could also be translated "a good wife means a good life."[9] Marriage is always a great risk, especially without God's guidance, but if you are fortunate enough to marry a companionable and talented wife, then praise God for being good to you.

Proverbs 19:14 echoes a similar theme: "House and wealth are inherited from parents, but a prudent wife is from the Lord." The laws of inheritance might ensure that a man would receive the family wealth, but marriage had no such human guarantee. Parents usually selected the marriage partner for their sons or daughters, but even with their greater experience and wisdom, they were not infallible. The risk is far greater in the modern world when young people choose whom they will marry, sometimes for the most superficial reasons. Human beings need the true wisdom that comes from the Lord.

The Joy of Marriage

Although the ancients approached marriage from more practical considerations, that did not mean they did not see the institution as inherently enjoyable. They could be quite frank about its pleasures. The book of Proverbs urged its male readers to enjoy the wife of their youth (Prov. 5:18). People married quite young, and the author probably means the phrase "wife of your youth" quite literally. If a couple lived into their 30s and 40s (most people died young)[10] and neither partner had as yet died,[11] it would naturally be tempting to daydream about another spouse.

Although a couple might not start out with the expectation of romance that modern couples have, they could grow quite close. Proverbs 2:16, 17 speaks of the "loose woman" "who forsakes the partner of her youth." The Hebrew word translated "partner" is *'allup,* a term indicating the closest of friends.[12] It also appears in Proverbs 16:28; 17:9; and Psalm 55:13.

The enjoyment that Proverbs 5:18, 19 recommends included the wife's physical charms. "May her breasts satisfy you at all times; may you be intoxicated always by her love" (verse 19). The Hebrew consonants for the word rendered "breasts" can also be read as "affection," but most translators prefer the traditional understanding. It echoes, for example, the physical delight the couple in the Song of Solomon found in each other as well as the physical affection of Isaac and Rebekah (Gen. 26:8).

Some might be shocked by the explicitness of such phraseology, but men and women in the ancient Near East did not share the false prudery that has too often crept into Christianity. Marriage might be more than sex, but sex was definitely a fundamental aspect of the relationship. The world today may be obsessed with sex, but that does not mean the drive is from the devil. One should focus those natural and God-implanted sexual yearnings on one's marriage partner.

Modern research has found that sex is a powerful bonding agent between a couple. Not only does it develop deep physical ties, but profound emotional and psychological ones as well.

They become *one* in all senses of the word, as God said they would in Genesis 2:24. But the same bonding can occur outside of marriage as Paul recognized when he asked, "Do you not know that whoever is united to a prostitute becomes one body with her?" (1 Cor. 6:16). He then quoted Genesis 2:24. Sexual bonding with another outside the boundaries of the marital commitment will lead only to disappointment and pain. To try to avoid such bonding by keeping a sexual relationship at a superficial level is equally destructive.

The book of Proverbs recognizes that the wife has a powerful role in making marriage a success or failure. "A good wife is the crown of her husband, but she who brings shame is like rottenness in his bones" (Prov. 12:4). She can strengthen or destroy a marriage, make it healthy or sick. A good wife and mother provides great stability for the family (Prov. 14:1). Husband and wife train the children together and ideally speak with one voice (Prov. 1:8, 9; 6:20).

Adultery

Marriage, to be successful, had to be carefully guarded. To survive in a precarious world, the people of the small towns and villages had to work closely together in the fields or on other projects. The genders had more contact with each other than one might expect. The seclusion of women in the home did not develop until later, and then primarily among the wealthy, who could afford servants to replace the labor of the isolated female members of the family. Thrown constantly together, people became infatuated with each other just as easily back then as they do today. In such a tightly knit society this could lead to especially disastrous results. A couple carrying on an affair could not simply move to another town. It would be difficult for the man to find work and almost impossible for the woman. As we have pointed out previously, people could survive only as part of an extended family. Women either had to have a family support them or had to turn to prostitution in order to survive.

In addition, as we mentioned in chapter 11, people did not travel as we do today. One could not start life with a new spouse at will. An adulterous couple had to remain where they were, and if they did that, it had the potential of tearing the community apart. That is one reason Israelite law dealt so harshly with adultery.[13] The death of those involved would hopefully lance the festering wounds of offended pride[14] and broken relationships and thus prevent the incident from triggering a blood feud. Adultery could tear whole communities apart as each side sought to preserve its honor. While adultery in the modern world might not lead to such a dramatic response, its effects can be more subtle and equally damaging in the long run.

Sexual infidelity distorted God's intended relationship between man and woman. It wasted powers that God had provided to make a close family (Prov. 5:9-23). In the process it substituted a false, superficial intimacy for a stable one that could emerge only in marriage (verses 19, 20). Men and women forfeited their honor (verse 9; Prov. 6:23) and freedom (Prov. 23:27, 28) when they sought sex outside of the commitment of marriage. They threw away the best years of their lives (Prov. 5:9, 11) and perhaps even their possessions (Prov. 6:26; 29:3), especially dangerous in a world of limited resources. Sexual immorality was social suicide, leading to disgrace (Prov. 6:32-35). And that shame would spill over onto their families. Adultery amounted to a spiritual death wish (Prov. 2:18, 19).

The book of Proverbs had much to say about the need to protect both the family and the community from adultery. Naturally it sees things from a male viewpoint.[15] Passages such as Proverbs 2:16-19;[16] 5:1-13, 18-20; 6:23-33;[17] and 7:4-27 warn of the adulterous woman (but not the adulterous man). Although, as we saw earlier, such passages operate on more than one level, and while cautioning against pursuing false wisdom, they speak in the imagery of marriage relationships and present concrete advice on how to avoid inappropriate relationships.

Proverbs has more to say than simply to advise avoidance of

the temptation of a relationship with a woman outside of marriage. It also presents a positive emphasis. A man should find sexual pleasure with his own wife (Prov. 5:15-18). Although one might get the impression that biblical writers usually considered the woman primarily at fault in sexual affairs, Proverbs 6:25 recognizes that the man has a responsibility too. He must watch over his "heart," which means more than just the emotions as we employ the imagery today. As mentioned before, in the ancient world the heart also stood for what we would call the mind—the reasoning faculties. In fact, it implied the whole personality.[18] To avoid temptation, a person must guard all that he or she is. Modern psychological studies have confirmed the biblical observation. Adultery irreparably damages who we are. The scars go deep into the personality as well as warp our relationships with others.

Interestingly, the tempter in Proverbs often uses religion as an excuse for her adulterous behavior (see Prov. 7:14). Even religion can be distorted into a justification for breaking the sacred boundaries of intimate relationships. We have seen this happen repeatedly in Christian cults as well as non-Christian religions.

The person who seeks a happy marriage must base it on fidelity—to the marriage partner, to the relationships of others, and to God Himself. Biblical religion arises from a covenant both between God and humanity and between fellow human beings. True wisdom, from the perspective of the book of Proverbs, includes protecting and nourishing all God-ordained relationships, especially marriage.

Even if marriage avoids adultery, it can stumble in other ways. If nothing else, it can degenerate from joy and pleasure to irritation and frustration. And that can easily turn into hatred. The death of a marriage can begin with quarrelsomeness. Proverbs 21:9 observes that "it is better[19] to live in a corner of the housetop than in a house shared with a contentious wife."[20]

The husband spreading his thin sleeping mat on the earthen roof among the household pots, jars, and implements stored there and sleeping by himself in the chilly night air or the damp rainy season presents a pitiful sight. The village men must have shaken their heads either in sympathy or scorn, and the women would have gossiped about the couple's problems. His heartache was in full public view. Yet the writer regards it as less frustrating than sharing the cramped quarters inside the tiny house with a scolding wife.

In a culture obsessed with issues of honor and shame,[21] it must have indeed been humiliating for the whole village to know what he was enduring. He could not hide it in the privacy of his home. Privacy was almost nonexistent in biblical society, and people who hid things were suspect, thus their neighbors would pry into their lives even more.

Proverbs 27:15 compares a contentious wife to water leaking through a mud roof. As the cold rainy season storms lashed against the house, the man could find no dry place to escape the constant dripping. The drops beating on his head or the unending patter of their falling eroded his sanity. In time the wait for the next drop to fall could become an even more excruciating torture. And this is what the man's marriage had degenerated to.

The ceaseless nagging of an unhappy wife could not only destroy happiness and self-respect, but also the marriage itself. While the book of Proverbs speaks of the results of an unhappy wife, all that the book has said applies equally to men. A loud, demanding husband can be just as destructive to the marriage relationship.

The "Ode to a Capable Wife"

Besides the problems and dangers of marriage, the book also dramatizes its wonderful possibilities. Proverbs 31:10-31 portrays the ideal through its "Ode to a Capable Wife," or as other translations phrase it, "A Virtuous Wife" or "Woman of Valor."

The passage is an acrostic poem, the first letters of each of its 22 couplets following the regular order of the Hebrew alphabet.[22] It develops in concrete detail the theme of Proverbs 18:22. The capable woman in chapter 31 is hardly a wife in the mold of 1950s American television programs. One could more correctly call her a corporate executive. She is clearly the spouse of a wealthy man, who would have an extended family consisting of both relatives and servants with their families. Since women took care of all the responsibilities within the home, she would be in charge of supervising a large and varied group of people. In addition, she managed several cottage industries.

For example, she was involved in manufacturing clothing, making more than enough for even her large family and selling them in the community (verse 24). She had to select the raw materials of wool and linen (verse 13), then weave (verse 19) and dye the fabric (verses 21, 22) and handle the sales (through bartering in the town market). During a period of history when most people possessed only one or two changes of garments, clothing was a valuable item. A shopper could not go to a nearby mall to pick up the latest style. People wore clothing and passed it down until it literally fell apart. Then they tore it into rags for other needs. Even the simplest garment was expensive and time-consuming to make. This explains the high value Scripture places on clothing in such stories as Judges 14 and in Jesus' concern for clothing the naked or His allusion to moths eating personal possessions.

Modern Westerners worry about cleaning out their too-full closets, but in Bible times the woman of Proverbs 31 manufactured a consumer item that was comparable in expense to a modern automobile. Beyond that, she also handled international trade (verses 14, 18) and real estate dealings (verse 16). (Remember, land was the fundamental unit of wealth in ancient society.) She was also active in community affairs, aiding the needy (verse 20). In the biblical world such help was the only thing that kept those without families from starving to death.

In her own home she would feed a large household and assign the countless tasks for the servant girls (verse 15). Another of her duties was being in charge of the lighting in the home. Biblical houses had no windows to let in illumination. Without glass, any openings had to be small to keep heat in and the cold out during the rainy winter season. Houses were dark day and night. The housewife kept small clay oil lamps (tiny enough to rest on the palm of the hand) burning at all hours. Because the lamps did not hold much olive oil, she had to wake up periodically during the night to refill them (verse 18). One commentator has compared her responsibility for the oil lamps to being in charge of the family gas and oil credit card.

The wife's skills and efforts not only aided the family, but, according to verse 23, allowed her husband to take a more active role in community affairs. He could take his place among the elders at the city gate. The gate was the main arena of business, judicial, and other civil activities. It was city hall, courthouse, and business office all rolled into one.[23] Thus the husband was not just loafing or gossiping there, but was an involved and prominent citizen.

Interestingly, the poem says little about raising children. While she had charge of them, they were not her responsibility alone. The whole extended family participated in their care.

Although the wife in the poem was perhaps more successful than some of her contemporaries, everything that the passage describes fell within the normal range of an Israelite woman's duties. While women's roles sometimes placed them somewhat behind the scenes, they were hardly passive. They had to be strong and carried great responsibilities. The biblical housewife was not just a cook, baby-sitter, and general servant. She was an equal with her husband. In her home she had complete charge of what went on,[24] including its finances, and raised the children. Boys lived in a totally female-dominated world until about age 7 or 8, when they had to make a traumatic adjustment to the world of men.[25] Thus the wife had a powerful influence on the whole family.

Unlike the rest of the book of Proverbs, the husband hardly makes an appearance. He just admires the wife as an infinitely valuable gift from the Lord (verse 10).[26] Clearly she is a role model for even the most modern career woman.

But she is even more than that.

Kathleen M. O'Connor has suggested that the wife of Proverbs 31 was "a summary of the whole book of Proverbs" because the book's central character is Wisdom Woman herself.[27] "Marry this woman," O'Connor sees the book as urging its readers. "Live your entire life in her shadow, as her child and beloved. Become a member of her household. If you do this, you will gain every human fulfillment."[28]

Roland Murphy asks if we should see the woman of Proverbs 31 in the Woman of Wisdom of the first part of the book, then comments: "One is left with an eerie feeling of identity: both Woman Wisdom and the woman of valor are into house-building (cf. Prov. 9:1; 14:1); both influence the public, and both are associated with the fear of the Lord."[29]

Marriage should reflect among human beings how the members of the Godhead love among Themselves. The Bible often shows the "masculine" side of such love through the image of God as our Father and Husband. But being female also reflects the image of God (Gen. 1:27). The Bible employs feminine imagery to portray the Divine. Just as Jesus depicted what God is like through a woman in Luke 15:8-10, so Proverbs 31:10-31 hints at what God is like through the illustration of a capable woman. She shows through her life the benefits God would like to shower upon us, the kinds of love and help the Godhead longs to give us. And no greater honor could be given any woman than to be chosen to depict the Divine.

---

[1] For helpful background on the family in the Old Testament, see Leo G. Perdue, Joseph Blenkinsopp, John J. Collins, and Carol Meyers, *Families in Ancient Israel* (Louisville, Ky.: Westminster Press, 1997).

[2] Bruce J. Malina and Richard L. Rohrbaugh, *Social-Science Commentary on the Gospel of John*, p. 70.

[3] See Malina and Rohrbaugh, *Social-Science Commentary on the Synoptic Gospels*, pp. 30, 241.

[4] *International Standard Bible Encyclopedia*, vol. 2, pp. 694, 695.

[5] Malina and Rohrbaugh, p. 89.

[6] ———, *Synoptic Gospels,* pp. 348, 349.

[7] Derek Kidner, *Proverbs,* p. 130.

[8] Roland E. Murphy, *Proverbs,* p. 138.

[9] R.B.Y. Scott, *Proverbs/Ecclesiastes,* p. 114.

[10] I have discussed the length of life span elsewhere. See Gerald Wheeler, *Beyond Life: What God Says About Life, Death, and Immortality,* pp. 113, 114.

[11] At least a quarter of families had one or both parents dead by the time their children reached their early teens, a major reason the Bible is so concerned about orphans.

[12] Kidner, pp. 49, 50.

[13] See such laws as Leviticus 20:10 and Deuteronomy 22:22. We have no idea of how extensively biblical society enforced them, however.

[14] Malina and Rohrbaugh, *Synoptic Gospels,* p. 53.

[15] Scripture appears to define adultery almost exclusively as a sexual relationship between a married man and another man's wife, ignoring the relationship of a married man with an unmarried woman.

[16] The ancient Egyptian document *The Instruction of Ani* has an interesting parallel to verse 16.

[17] Passages in the Egyptian *Teachings of Ptah-Hotep* echo Proverbs 6:23-29. See Victor H. Matthews and Don C. Benjamin, *Old Testament Parallels,* p. 187.

[18] *Dictionary of Biblical Imagery,* pp. 368, 369; Malina and Rohrbaugh, *Synoptic Gospels,* pp. 53, 226, 227, 356.

[19] "It is better" is one of the favorite stylistic devices of the book of Proverbs.

[20] Verse 19 puts the unhappy husband in the inhospitable desert.

[21] See Malina and Rohrbaugh, pp. 76, 77, 213, 214, 309-311.

[22] Some acrostic poems in the Hebrew Scriptures follow a variant sequence of the alphabet. Archaeologists have found this same order on some pottery shards that students were practicing the alphabet on.

[23] *Dictionary of Biblical Imagery,* pp. 321, 322.

[24] Perhaps part of the reasons behind Potiphar's wife's seduction of Joseph was hostility toward him because he had usurped her role of being in charge of the household.

[25] Malina and Rohrbaugh, *Synoptic Gospels,* p. 300; *Gospel of John,* pp. 272, 273.

[26] One cynical scholar has suggested that the poem was propaganda to use on Israelite men attracted to non-Israelite women. Why would anyone want to marry them after reading the "Ode to a Capable Woman"?

[27] Kathleen M. O'Connor, *The Wisdom Literature* (Wilmington, Del.: Michael Glazier, 1988), p. 77.

[28] *Ibid.,* p. 79.

[29] Murphy, *Proverbs,* p. 248.

Chapter Thirteen

DIVINE AND HUMAN PARENTING: THE PATH TO TRUE DISCIPLINE

Parental Discipline

One of the best known and most controversial sayings in the book of Proverbs is Proverbs 13:24: "Those who spare the rod hate their children, but those who love them are diligent to discipline them." The concept of corporal punishment has been widespread throughout history and among almost every culture. Egyptian schoolboys as they learned to read and write had to copy such passages as: "Boys have their ears on their backsides: they listen when they are beaten." The supposed testimony of a student to his former teacher claimed: "You caned me, and so your teaching entered my ear."[1] The Assyrian document *The Teachings of Ahiqar* states simply: "Spare the rod, spoil the child."[2] Much of the world has assumed that children need physical punishment, and ancient Israel shared the widespread belief.

Proverbs 19:18 declares, "Discipline your children while there is hope; do not set your heart on their destruction." "Do not withhold discipline from your children; if you beat them with a rod, they will not die" (Prov. 23:13). Beating the children will deliver them from death (verse 14).

The proverb has become controversial in North America

because of a widespread misuse of the concept. People can distort their right to discipline, turning it into abuse, and cite Scripture as justification. In the New Testament, Hebrews 12:5-11 supports the duties of parents to discipline their children and employs the concept as an analogy for how God trains His children so that we may share His holiness (verse 10). It seems painful at the time, the biblical writer recognizes, but ultimately it produces righteousness in us (verse 11). Sadly, though, all things, including discipline, can be warped. As a consequence, Ephesians 6:4 cautions fathers not to incite anger in their children as they discipline them.

Because so many parents have distorted their responsibility to discipline into just plain abuse, governmental agencies and educational institutions in some areas have prohibited corporal punishment, including spanking. In the United States conservative Christians have regarded such restrictions as an attack on their Christian beliefs. It has become a hotly contested issue. If you listen to the rhetoric of some Christians, you would think that God had commanded parents to beat their children within an inch of their lives.

Scripture, especially the book of Proverbs, feels that physical punishment is a legitimate part of good parenting. It takes more than mere words to remove the folly that creeps into children (Prov. 22:15). Discipline must begin early and continue throughout childhood. It, along with everything else that happens during those formative years, will shape children for the rest of their lives. "Train children in the right way, and when old, they will not stray" (verse 6). But we must always remember that discipline is not magical.

Both children and adults can refuse to accept its lessons, but it will still have shaped their lives more than they realize. Some, of course, will choose to "despise" discipline and will unfortunately reap the consequences of their decision (Prov. 5:12-14). But those who accept instruction and discipline will find understanding and wisdom (Prov. 15:32, 33). To neglect disciplining a child will lead only to shame for the parent (Prov. 29:15). In the biblical world, as is sadly even more true today, mothers did most of the child raising. At least biblical children had more exposure to their fathers, since the whole family worked together both in the fields and at home.[3]

Discipline Is a Community Affair

As we attempt to implement the biblical call for discipline, we must always keep in mind that such discipline took place within the extended family. It was not angry and frustrated parents versus the child. All adults in the household would be involved in the discipline. And the children always knew that they were loved and accepted by the entire extended family—relatives and servants as well, if the family had any.

If the child felt insecure or frightened, he or she could flee into the arms of a whole group of adults. The extended family would also both reinforce the parent's discipline of the child through group presence, and if such discipline veered into abuse, others could put pressure on the adult to temper the punishment. Neighbors, who knew everything that went on within the confines of the small communities, would also add their influence, either supporting the parent or shaming him or her if the discipline became too severe.

Today's nuclear (and increasingly single-parent) families often do not provide the emotional support to strengthen or restrain physical punishment. As a result it is much easier for discipline to get out of hand and turn into abuse. Such abuse has triggered the limitation of corporal punishment that has so upset conservative Christians.

Many parents experienced abusive discipline when they grew up, and when they find themselves under pressure or frustrated with their children, they revert to the only kind of parenting they have known. The increasing recognition of such abusive discipline has led to a strong reaction against such harsh child raising during the middle of the twentieth century.

Unfortunately, many parents swung to the other extreme. They did not give their children the discipline they needed. Society has been paying a heavy price as a result. But reverting to harsh discipline will not solve the problem either.

The biblical model is discipline within a loving and caring extended family. As already pointed out, such families included not only physical relatives, but also the immediate community. Today the church would be a major part of the biblical concept of the extended family. Church bodies and organizations can be as vital in raising a child as its biological or legal guardians. A congregation's members can help provide adult role models to meet the needs of children who have a missing parent or who lack aunts, uncles, or grandparents.

Scriptural discipline rejects abuse or harshness. The book of Proverbs "tacitly condemns the martinet by its own reasonable approach, its affectionate earnestness, and its assumption that the old find their natural crown, and the young their proper pride, in each other (17:6). The parents' chief resource is constructive, namely their 'law,' taught with loving persistence. This 'law' *(tora)* is a wide term which includes commands (cf. 3:1; 7:2) but is not confined to them: basically it means direction, and its aim here is to foster wise habits of thought and action (in the 'heart' and in the 'fingers,' 7:3 [as we have seen before, such imagery would stand for how we think and what we do]) which, so far from enslaving a person, will equip him to find his way through life with sureness (3:23; 4:12) and honour (1:9; 4:8, 9). There is a childhood reminiscence of its tenderness preserved in 4:3ff., and a sample of its bracing outspokenness, its home truths, in 31:1-9."[4]

According to Scripture, parental discipline of children is far more than physical punishment. It is how the parents—in fact, the whole extended family—live and treat each other. Every person in the family is a role model who shows the rest of the family what kind of persons they should be. With the disappearance of the extended family and the absence of one or even both parents, corporal punishment cannot possibly make up for the lack of the rest of the family's (and community's) discipline.

What Discipline Can't Do

Sometimes pastors and church members use Proverbs 22:6 in ways that bring cruel and needless guilt to struggling parents. One pastor proclaimed in a sermon that no child trained rightly would ever rebel or leave the church. When grieving parents whose children had abandoned their faith confronted the minister about his statement, he found himself forced to apologize. The next week he said in his sermon that he had not meant to hurt anybody—then added that he thought he was still right!

In a universe that God endowed with free will, created beings can choose to turn from good to evil. God, the most perfect of all parents, lost Lucifer and those angels who followed him. Human parents cannot expect perfect success no matter how carefully they discipline their children. Even perfect discipline does not automatically produce perfect children.

The book of Proverbs gives a number of reasons even the best discipline may fail. The scoffer refuses to listen (Prov. 13:1). You can't teach people when they think they know best[5] or when they tune out what you say. The wisdom tradition often equated "hearing" with "obeying."[6] To hear or listen to counsel was to put it into practice. But you could do little with a person who refused to listen—who rejected everything you had to say.

An idler (Prov. 10:5) or a profligate (Prov. 29:3) can emerge from even the best homes. Children may choose to despise (Prov. 15:20), mock or scorn (Prov. 30:17), or curse[7] (verse 11; Prov. 20:20) their parents—even in a culture that both stressed identities based on whose child one was and powerfully upheld the honoring of one's parents. Children growing up in the biblical world considered it their natural duty to care for their aged parents. They would have found it hard to imagine never accepting the responsibility. But it was still possible even in that strong culture to rob parents and argue "that is no crime" (Prov. 28:24).

Some children would attack their fathers and throw their mothers out of their homes (Prov. 19:26). To expel parents, especially mothers, was to consign them to death, since they could not survive on their own. Yet despite even the best discipline, such offspring could still reject everything their world stood for.

A Choice Each Must Make

Each of us decides what we will do about wisdom and the discipline it will bring to our lives. We must choose of our own free will to pursue wisdom (Prov. 2:2-4). It will never overwhelm us against our will. God alone is its only source (verses 6-9), but He cannot bestow it on those who refuse to accept it. The biblical sage does everything he can to get his readers to search for wisdom and its discipline. He urges us to be attentive to what he says (Prov. 4:20; 5:1). Listen to your parents, he pleads, and seek wisdom (Prov. 23:22-25). If we do, not only will we be happy, but also it will bring honor and joy to our parents, who have tried to bring us up right (verses 24, 25).[8]

God's Discipline

Not only do our parents discipline us to prepare us for life, but so also does God. "My child, do not despise the Lord's discipline or be weary of his reproof, for the Lord reproves the one he loves, as a father the son in whom he delights" (Prov. 3:11, 12). As we saw earlier, Hebrews 12:5-11 takes up this theme.

The problem of suffering is a complex one. Only in Proverbs 3:11, 12 does the book of Proverbs touch on it.[9] As even the sage observed: "No wisdom, no understanding, no counsel, can avail against the Lord" (Prov. 21:30). God's ways are ultimately beyond human comprehension. Here we will focus only on how response to divine discipline in a positive way can benefit our lives.

Most frequently the book shows the goals of divine discipline by contrasting the fool, who rejects wisdom and discipline, with the wise person, who accepts it (Prov. 12:1, 15; 13:18; 15:8-12; 21:27; 28:9). Interestingly, several of these passages (Prov. 15:8; 21:27; 28:9) mention things the believer should do, but in these situations God rejects them because they were done for the wrong reason. The book of Proverbs is interested in the motivations behind our actions as well as the deeds themselves. The prophets, and later Jesus, would go deeper into the true reasons behind our religious practice and behavior. Our choice is to permit God to purge our characters of their dross by willingly responding to His discipline. We can of our free will allow Him to shape our characters into His image, or, in the words of Proverbs 29:1, we can become like "one who is often reproved, yet remains stubborn, [and] will suddenly be broken beyond healing."

❧ ❧ ❧

Throughout this book we have been seeking wisdom. We have seen that wisdom is not just intellectual knowledge or even necessarily religious behavior. Nor is it just doing the right thing the right way. Rather, wisdom is the fear of the Lord—our relationship to a God who leaves us in awe as much as He fills us with love. He is the God who made and sustains the universe and will forever be beyond our total comprehension. We recognize that He created all there is and makes it work as it should. The God of the Bible is order and righteousness far beyond the *maat* of the Egyptians or the wisdom that any of the ancients sought. True wisdom escapes even modern scientific inquiry. It is a loving dependence on God Himself and a reflection of His character.

> "Trust in the Lord with all your heart,
>   and do not rely on your insight.
> In all your ways acknowledge him,
>   and he will make straight your paths.
> Do not be wise in your own eyes;
>   fear the Lord, and turn away from evil.
> It will be a healing for your flesh
>   and a refreshment for your body" (Prov. 3:5-8).

[1] Cited in R. N. Whybray, *The Book of Proverbs*, p. 80.

[2] Victor H. Matthews and Don C. Benjamin, *Old Testament Parallels*, p. 179.

[3] See Leo G. Perdue, Joseph Blenkinsopp, John J. Collins, and Carol Meyers, *Families in Ancient Israel* for a detailed look at family life in the Old Testament world, and Carolyn Osick and David L. Balch, *Families in the New Testament World: Households and Home Churches* (Louisville, Ky.: Westminster John Knox, 1997) for the later biblical period.

[4] Derek Kidner, *Proverbs*, p. 51.

[5] Whybray, p. 77.

[6] Roland E. Murphy, *Proverbs*, p. 95.

[7] It is the same phrase used in Exodus 21:17, a passage that calls for the death of those who curse their parents (Whybray, p. 115). "The metaphor of the lamp [in Proverbs 20:20] stands for the fate of the one who curses. The lamp of life will be extinguished" (Murphy, *Proverbs*, p. 152).

[8] Kidner cites the commentator Delitzsch as seeing the joy a wise son brings as a motif that begins each major paragraph of the central portion of the book, such as Proverbs 10:1, 13:1, and 15:20 (Kidner, p. 52).

[9] For a discussion of this issue from the perspective of the wisdom tradition, see Murphy, *Proverbs*, pp. 261-269, and the many commentaries on the book of Job, also a part of biblical wisdom literature.